# 100 THINGS TO DO IN TEXAS BEFORE YOU DIE

2nd Edition

Padre Island National Seashore
Photo courtesy of E. R. Bills

# 100 THINGS TO DO IN TEXAS BEFORE YOU DIE

2nd Edition

E.R. BILLS

REEDY PRESS

Reedy Press
PO Box 5131
St. Louis, MO 63139, USA
www.reedypress.com



Library of Congress Control Number: 2022942711

ISBN: 9781681064185

Design by Jill Halpin
Cover photo: Courtesy Getty Images
Interior photos:
Page 40, Image courtesy of Jay Gannett, https://www.flickr.com/photos/29531805@N07/46229796741/, licensed under https://creativecommons.org/licenses/by-sa/2.0/.
Page 62, Image courtesy of Forest Kastch, https://commons.wikimedia.org/wiki/File:SpaceX_Starship_SN8_launch_as_viewed_from_South_Padre_Island.jpg#filehistory, licensed under https://creativecommons.org/licenses/by-sa/4.0/deed.en.
Pages 90-91, Image courtesy of Mark Bonica, https://www.flickr.com/photos/23119666@N03/13317751955/, licensed under https://creativecommons.org/licenses/by-sa/2.0/.
Page 156, Image courtesy of Thomas Shahan, https://www.flickr.com/photos/49580580@N02/29849531957/, licensed under https://creativecommons.org/licenses/by-sa/2.0/.

Printed in the United States of America
22 23 24 25 26 5 4 3 2 1

# DEDICATION

This book is dedicated to my parents,
E. R. Bills Sr. and Rebecca Sue Bills.
They gave me a big head start.

Courtyard of the Hotel Paisano in Marfa
Photo courtesy of Wikimedia Commons

# CONTENTS

**Parks and Recreation**

**History and Culture**

Author at McKittrick Springs in the Guadalupe Mountains
Photo courtesy of E. R. Bills

# FOREWORD

Here it is, the second edition or, as we say in Texas, the first overtime period. The game isn't over yet, and this edition is simply the sequel's coin toss, except the coin, once again, has 100 sides. Where will your next adventure land you?

—E. R. Bills
November 1, 2022

# PREFACE

When you get right down to it, there's no way of avoiding criticism for limiting a premortem bucket list of "things to do in Texas before you die" to a measly 100. Steinbeck was correct when he asserted that "Texas is the obsession, the proper study, and the passionate possession of all Texans," and anyone who's lived here 10 years can easily rattle off a hundred things they'd like to do before they finish their lunch break.

The challenge, then, is looking over the entire state and narrowing down which settings and activities are the most germane in terms of Texas culture or a true Texas experience. This does not mean ranking activities around the state with an eye on their popularity or how easy they are to reach. A hard look is required, and even then it's tough to narrow down what's intrinsically Lone Star.

I am a native Texan and have resided in Texas all my life. I began traveling the state early. When I was 12, my father took my younger brother and me on an eight-day canoe trek down the Lower Canyons of the Rio Grande, and the experience has never left me. For the past 20 years or so, I've explored almost every corner of the state myself, at times solo, with my wife, with my wife and kids, and sometimes just with the children. We've gotten muddy on wild cave tours, ventured down the entire length of the 60-mile Padre Island National Seashore, shared a beach with a nesting Kemp's ridley sea turtle, witnessed the Perseid meteor shower while standing in the South Llano River, attended the Ghost Walk in Jefferson, snuck down the Ghost Road of Saratoga, had the Devil's River all to ourselves, seen black bears in the Big Bend, stumbled across secret weapons at the Devil's Sinkhole, kept time with Cassiopeia at the McDonald Observatory, examined the Buried City in the Panhandle, leaped off limestone cliffs at Inks Lake, navigated Caddo Lake, drove the free golf carts around Fort Griffin, braved the City Tube Chute in New Braunfels (without a tube), petted stingrays at the Texas State Aquarium, and been emphatically warned by the heart-stopping hiss of a mama alligator at Sea Rim. We've defeated electronica for significant spells, confounded GPS, gone days without a cell phone signal, and wandered into places where it seemed there wasn't another human being for a hundred miles. We've explored our home state with vim and vigor and had countless epiphanies, revelations, and breathtaking moments of sheer, unbridled joy at the breadth, depth, and diversity of this place, which is why I feel comfortable attempting this list.

—E. R. Bills
August 1, 2018

Author hanging cell phone over edge of boardwalk to take picture at Gambusia Trail in Sea Rim State Park
Photo courtesy of E. R. Bills

# ACKNOWLEDGMENTS

Special thanks to the family, friends, and fellow Texans who inspired or informed my travels or helped me put this volume together, including my wife, Stacie; my children; Alta and Johnnie Kettler, Ron Howell, Stephen Barnes, William Michael Smith, Wednesday Tijerina, Billy Huckaby, Kathy Hudson, Scott Conner, David Martin Davies, Wes Ferguson, Robert "Bob" Joseph Protus, Joe Vano, Eric Edwards and Maria Cristina Hernandez, and too many others to name.

Sign for Luckenbach, Texas, a dot of a place in Gillespie County, Texas
Photo courtesy of Carol M. Highsmith America/Library of Congress

# AMUSEMENTS AND ENTERTAINMENT

1

# MINGLE
## IN MARFA

Ever wonder what a meeting between hipster bohemians and West Texas might look like? The quaint little town of Marfa says "Hold my beer."

The 88-year-old Hotel Paisano is now a rendezvous point for starched-jean ranch hands and globe-trotting South Americans, Asians, Europeans, and others . . . all in search of a latte on the frontier. Throw in a thrift store (the only one for a hundred miles in any direction), several Manhattan-priced art galleries, a food truck, and El Cosmico—a hostel-like spread of community accommodations that offer space in trailers, tepees, yurts, and a 3,800-square-foot apartment on the second floor of the Brite Building downtown (for large group rental)—and this town delivers an inimitable atmosphere of quirkiness that serves as an entertaining break from conventional Big Bend fare. Sometimes you get the feeling the place is full of folks who wanted to visit West Texas but not really be in West Texas, but that's okay.

There are coffee shops, a great public library, hip taco trucks, rustic bars, random beer gardens, and the fickle Marfa Lights. Regardless, this place is a Lone Star parfait you must try at least once.

visitmarfa.com

## 2

# LINGER

## AT LUCKENBACH

There's no greater testament to the power of a country song than the tiny Hill Country community of Luckenbach. Founded in the mid-19th century and virtually a ghost town by the early 1970s, Luckenbach was a place folks saw no reason to stop in for decades. But then Waylon Jennings (who'd never been to Luckenbach) and Willie Nelson recorded and released "Luckenbach, Texas (Back to the Basics of Love)," and bingo! A speck on the map with only three permanent residents was transformed into one of the epicenters of the country music universe.

And it remains so today.

If you call yourself a Texan, it's hard to argue against a pilgrimage to Luckenbach at your earliest convenience. The town's two remaining businesses are the general store (which moonlights as a saloon and post office) and the dance hall. The general store is a good place to grab a beer and pick out a souvenir—it sells Luckenbach bumper stickers, ball caps, bandannas, patio bricks, coffee mugs, and coozies. The store's website features a busy events calendar all year round and has a link to the monthly *Luckenbach Moon* newsletter, where you can survey a month-to-month schedule of upcoming musical acts and general goings on.

412 Luckenbach Town Loop, Fredericksburg, TX 78624
(830) 997-3224, luckenbachtexas.com

3

# REVERE

## THE SAN ANTONIO RIVER WALK

Now comprising 15 miles of pedestrian paths that hug the San Antonio River's edge, the River Walk stretches from the community's art center to its fabulous Spanish Missions, which are a must-see in their own right. Shaded by the surrounding buildings, the river winds through the busy downtown commerce area, plied by colorful cruise barges and tour-guide gondoliers. The spectacle gives San Antonio one of the best downtowns in America and easily the best in Texas. There's nothing else quite like it.

When you get down to S. Presa Street, detour north to visit the McNutt Sculpture Garden of the Briscoe Western Art Museum, and check out the Briscoe's interior space, which features several unexpected artifacts, including Santa Anna's sword and Pancho Villa's saddle.

thesanantonioriverwalk.com

### INTREPID TEXAN

A 15-minute drive south, the Texas Air Museum at Stinson Municipal Airport is worth a visit. San Antonio is considered the birthplace of U.S. military aviation, and the two barn-burning Stinson sisters, Katherine and Marjorie, trained dozens of American and Canadian men to fly combat missions in World War I—but weren't allowed to join the fight themselves. Our loss!

4

# GET WET
## AT THE TEXAS STATE AQUARIUM

The largest aquarium in Texas and one of the largest in the United States, the Texas State Aquarium may be the best attraction to visit on the entire Gulf Coast. A self-supporting, nonprofit institution dedicated to promoting environmental conservation and the rehabilitation of wildlife in the Gulf of Mexico, the facility is located at the southernmost tip of the bayside Corpus Christi Beach.

Ever petted a shark before?

What about a starfish or a stingray?

Visitors can get up close and personal with all sorts of sea life here, including sea otters, sea turtles, groupers, tuna, and invertebrate Medusozoa—jellyfish. The big fish tank is stunning, and the vertical tank jellyfish exhibits are practically otherworldly. A small water park is also out front for young folks.

2710 N. Shoreline Blvd., Corpus Christi, TX 78402
(800) 477-4853, texasstateaquarium.org

### INTREPID TEXAN

The Mirador de la Flor, a monument to slain Tejano music superstar Selena Quintanilla Perez, sits just a few minutes away at 600 N. Shoreline Blvd.

5

# TAKE IN A RODEO

When Greenville native Audie Murphy—the most decorated American soldier of World War II—was asked about the true meaning of America, he gave a short list of things that he thought summed us up. The list ended with the sound of children laughing, a newspaper, a political rally, and a policeman's badge. The list started with a Texas rodeo.

A Texas rodeo may or may not encapsulate the true meaning of America, but it definitely captures some of the authentic essence of the Lone Star state. Texas wasn't an easy place to live in the old days, and it wasn't for the faint of heart. The early residents and settlers—of all backgrounds—were hardscrabble, tough customers. They had to be. The desolate frontier was an unpredictable, unforgiving place, and the modern rodeo still celebrates the pioneer side of our forebears' hardships.

**West of the Pecos Rodeo (last weekend in June)**
The real deal and attracts professional rodeo cowboys from all over the country.

Pecos, TX
www.pecosrodeo.com

**Texas Cowboy Reunion (usually late June or early July)**
**Known as the "World's Largest Amateur Rodeo"**

620 N. Swenson St., Stamford, TX 79553
texascowboyreunion.com

**Stockyards Championship Rodeo (weekly)**
Held every Friday and Saturday night, the world's first indoor rodeo and only year-round rodeo.

Cowtown Coliseum
121 E. Exchange Ave., Fort Worth, TX 76164
stockyardsrodeo.com

**San Antonio Stock Show & Rodeo (in February)**
One of the largest rodeos in the world.

723 AT&T Center Parkway, San Antonio, TX 78219
sarodeo.com

**Houston Livestock Show & Rodeo**
**(late February through mid-March)**
Another one of the largest rodeos in the world.

NRG Pkwy, Houston, TX
rodeohouston.com

6

# STROLL ALONG
## THE GALVESTON SEAWALL

Morning, noon, or night, the seawall in Galveston is a Lone Star marvel. Almost 17 feet tall and 16 feet thick (at the base), this protective barrier runs for more than 10 miles. The mainland side is lined with restaurants, hotels, bars, and souvenir shops, and the beach side is occasionally intersected by a jetty or fishing pier. Intermittent stairs allow access to the beach and Gulf of Mexico, but the sidewalk path on the wall gives you a view of it all—wall, beach, water, and so much more. It's a beautiful pedestrian byway that's sure to inspire some beautiful memories.

At the intersection of 25th St. and Seawall Blvd., the Galveston Historic Pleasure Pier, which extends out over the ocean, is a perfect platform for carnival games, several rides, a small roller coaster, and a large Ferris wheel.

### INTREPID TEXAN

The Galveston downtown area has some real spunk. Check out the Strand District, Bishop's Palace, the Nautical Antiques and Tropical Décor shop, and the Galveston Bookshop, and then grab a bite to eat at the wonderful, eclectic Mosquito Cafe.

7

# STEP ABOARD
## THE TEXAS STATE RAILROAD

Writer G. K. Chesterton once remarked that "The only way of catching a train I have ever discovered is to miss the train before." In the infancy of the new millennium, most Texans have missed the era of railroad travel by a few generations and will probably never be able to fully appreciate it for what it was, but we can still catch a glimpse in the Piney Woods of East Texas.

The Texas State Railroad has operated diesel and steam engines for more than 100 years old and makes runs from Rusk and Palestine on a regular basis, with several passenger options. You can travel in the Presidential Car and enjoy appetizers and complimentary champagne. For even more fun, you can travel in a Glass-Topped Dome car. Other options include First Class and Open-Air Coach (featuring vintage wooden seats). You can even join the engineer up front for a ride-along.

texasstaterailroad.net

### INTREPID TEXAN

The Redlands Hotel in Palestine is one of the neatest places to stay in Texas. Built in 1915, it has a top-notch restaurant, a cozy bar, and a third-floor courtyard.

8

# ATTEND
## A TEXAS FESTIVAL

This is a tough one because they come in all shapes, sizes, venues, and themes, and, in a place as big as Texas, you have hundreds to choose from. From SXSW, the Batfest, and Winnie the Pooh's buddy Eeyore's Birthday—all in Austin—to a celebration of salt in Grand Saline, a Stone Age Fair in Perryton, a Watermelon Thump Festival in Luling, a Peach Festival in Weatherford, a Hatch Chile Fest in Grand Prairie, a Strawberry Festival in Poteet, a Kolache Fest in Hallettsville, a Cheeseburger Festival in Friona, a Fiddlers Fest in San Patricio, a Balloon Festival in Plano, an Anime Fest in Dallas, a Rose Festival in Tyler, a film festival in Nacogdoches, and the Charro Days Festival in Brownsville, the Lone Star state has something to satiate every festival fetish.

**Wurstfest (New Braunfels)**

Wurstfest is one of the grandest celebrations of German culture in the US, bringing together all kinds of Texans with generations of their German neighbors. For 10 consecutive days, folks pour into Comal County community's Landa Park to fill their steins with German beer and consume copious amounts of German sausage. There's wurst stew, wurst on a stick, sauerkraut, deep-fried sauerkraut balls, strudels, *kartoffelpuffer* (potato pancakes), and Polka music.

The first Wurstfest in 1961 attracted 2,000 people. Today, the event attracts more than 100,000 participants. Bring a hardy appetite and your favorite pair of Lederhosen. *Sprechen Sie Fun?*

wurstfest.com

**Kerrville Folk Festival (Kerrville)**

The Kerrville Folk Festival is the longest continuously running music festival in North America and the pulse of the songwriting community in Texas and beyond. For 18 straight days and nights, the festival offers concerts and activities that nurture and develop artistic expression for attendees of all ages, focused on nurturing and developing artistic expression, especially the art of songwriting.

kerrvillefolkfestival.org

**Great Texas Mosquito Festival (Clute)**

Since 1981, a 25-foot-tall inflatable mosquito dubbed Willie Man-Chew has presided over this raucous Brazoria County event that features contests, a carnival, live entertainment, and a 5K run.

mosquitofestival.com

**North Texas Book Festival (Denton)**

Since the turn of the new millennium, the NTBF has been one of the state's coolest literary events, and the festival proceeds promote literacy in the area.

ntbf.org

**Texas Sandfest (Port Aransas)**

Since 1997, the Sandfest has grown into the largest native-sand sculpture competition in the US, and the funds it raises are used to support local charities and college scholarships. You're gonna need a bigger sand bucket!

texassandfest.org

# TWO-STEP
## AT THE BROKEN SPOKE

Long before Austin was weird or anyone was even trying to keep it weird, the Broken Spoke was just country. Now that Austin is clearly becoming more corporate than weird, the Spoke, unaffected by the hipster chic springing up around it, is weirdly even more country.

A roadhouse dance hall that's probably one of the few places left in Austin where you can still really find Texas, the Spoke has hosted most of the country greats over the years, including Bob Wills and the Texas Playboys, Tex Ritter, Roy Acuff, Kitty Wells, Willie Nelson, Asleep at the Wheel, and George Strait, who appeared there once a month from 1975 to 1982. The 661-person-capacity venue still showcases old-time country music, serves good food and cold beer, and may be the best place to two-step in the state.

3201 S. Lamar Blvd., Austin, Texas 78704
(512) 442-6189, brokenspokeaustintx.net

### INTREPID TEXAN

Serious Texas music fans can catch *Austin City Limits Live at Moody Theater*. This recorded PBS event is the longest-running music program in television history.

310 West Willie Nelson Blvd., Austin, TX, 78701
(512) 225-7999, acltv.com

## OTHER LIVE MUSIC VENUES

**Gruene Hall**

Texas's oldest dance hall.

1281 Gruene Rd., New Braunfels, TX 78130
(830) 606-1281
www.gruenehall.com

**John T. Floore's Country Store**

Storied honky-tonk venue with BBQ and an outdoor stage.

14492 Old Bandera Rd., Helotes, TX 78023
(210) 695-8827
www.liveatfloores.com

**Cheatham Street Warehouse**

Laidback heavyweight that has hosted Willie Nelson, Jerry Jeff Walker, Townes Van Zandt, Marcia Ball, and many more. It also gave George Strait and the Ace in the Hole Band their first gig, booked Stevie Ray Vaughan for a long-running weekly appearance, and developed legendary alt-country folk artist Todd Snider.

119 Cheatham St., San Marcos, TX 78666
(512) 353-3777
www.cheathamstreet.com

**Silver Slipper**

As Texas historian and music writer Joe Nick Patoski puts it, "Places like this don't exist anymore, but you start to believe it will last forever." It probably won't, so get there on a Saturday night and witness masterful rhythm and blues performances while you still can.

3717 Crane St., Houston, TX 77026
(713) 673-9004

10

# VISIT
## A GHOST TOWN

Located in McCulloch County just north of the intersection of FM 765 and CR 22, the ghost town of Doole has a few overgrown structures left and the remains of a concrete stadium built on a hill. It's not exactly the Coliseum in Rome, but the crumbling cement bleachers are reminiscent of a Roman ruin. You have to watch your step there, however, because where gridiron gladiators once competed, rattlesnakes roam.

There's no getting around the growing urbanization of the Lone Star state, and this trend has been unmistakably detrimental to small towns, the traditional underpinnings of Texas culture. Love it or hate it, Texans have become citified, and the skeletal remains created by this inevitable phenomenon—ghost towns—will probably continue to multiply. They dot the state in every direction, and they're important to look upon as Texans reconcile who they were with what they're becoming. Some communities died overnight, and others took years to kill. Many were the result of unsustainable industrial development, and others suffered catastrophes. Some simply perished at the whim of a railroad route preference or highway planning. Regardless of the details, they are poignant reminders of things past and eloquent harbingers of things to come.

**Kent**

Located in Culberson County at the intersection of CR 2424 and Interstate 10, Kent is still on maps, but only an abandoned convenience store, a few empty houses, and the rock walls of a large, gutted public school remain.

**Independence**

The wealthiest community in the state in 1845, Independence was the original site of Baylor University and Sam Houston's home when he served as a U.S. senator. When town leaders refused to grant a right-of-way to the Santa Fe Railroad, it took its tracks elsewhere, and Independence began a slow decline. A few buildings and markers and four columns from the original Baylor University edifice still remain.

**Fodice**

Located in Houston County southeast of Crocket on CR 4200, the town's remains include a closed church, a collapsing school, and a cemetery. But it features prominently in a creepy short story titled "Crepuscular" in the inaugural volume of the annual *Road Kill: Texas Horror by Texas Writers* anthology.

**Tascosa**

Located in Oldham County just north of the intersection of U.S. Hwy. 385 and Ranch to Market Rd. 1061, Tascosa (or Old Tascosa) sprang up in the 1880s as a good stop on the way to Dodge City, Kansas. It briefly served as the capital of 10 Texas Panhandle counties and became a regional merchandising center for ranches within a 100-mile radius. The only two structures left are the remains of a crumbling rock schoolhouse (erected in 1889) and the old courthouse (now the Julius Bivens Museum), both of which are part of Cal Farley's Boys Ranch.

# STARGAZE
## AT THE MCDONALD OBSERVATORY

Commencing at an open-air amphitheater about a half-hour after sunset in the Davis Mountains, the Evening Star Parties at the McDonald Observatory (held Tuesdays, Fridays, and Saturdays, with additional nights added during peak season) are on the list of the coolest things to do in Texas. Resident astronomers use laser pointers to identify prominent stars, planets, and constellations in the night sky and then treat attendees to incredible views of galaxies, supernovas, and other celestial bodies in some of the observatory's high-powered telescopes. The observatory also offers daytime solar viewings and guided tours of the facility, and the Visitors Center includes exhibits, a theater, and a gift shop.

3640 Dark Sky Drive, Fort Davis, TX 79734
(432) 426-3640, mcdonaldobservatory.org

### INTREPID TEXAN

The Chihuahuan Desert Nature Center is just 20 miles away on State Hwy. 118. It's an excellent resource for examining regional flora.
cdri.org

# ATTEND
## THE STATE FAIR OF TEXAS

Staged at historic Fair Park on the outskirts of Dallas, the State Fair of Texas is an exciting sensory overload. The smell of fresh, deep-fried corny dogs (where they were actually invented); the culinary array of other deep-fried whatsits you're tempted to try after the corny dog; the clatter, laughter, and buzz of people playing games at the Texas-sized midway; the amusements and rides, including a roller coaster and the 20-story, 35-gondola Ferris wheel (the tallest in the state); a stock show and strange animal races; the cookoffs, the live music, and the wine garden; and Big Tex welcoming all, even after the Texas-OU game. Win or lose. The 24-day event was first held in 1886 and usually begins every year on the last Friday in September.

3921 Martin Luther King, Jr. Blvd., Dallas, TX 75210
(214) 565-9931, bigtex.com

### INTREPID TEXAN

If you have any energy left after the Fair, an interesting evening can be had in Deep Ellum, Dallas's eclectic, downtown entertainment district.
www.deepellumtexas.com

13

# WATCH
## YOUR FAVORITE PROFESSIONAL SPORTS TEAM PLAY

Like everywhere else in America, sports are a big deal in Texas, and most folks feel pretty strongly about their favorite teams at the professional and college levels. Even when wildly disparate Texans cannot, will not, and never agree on a single political or philosophical question, they become tight-knit, "take-a-bullet-for-you" brothers (or sisters) at the tailgate party on game day.

The Dallas Cowboys are still America's team. Houston is over the loss of the Oilers and embracing the Texans. The Houston Astros are an MLB powerhouse. The San Antonio Spurs have won five NBA championships and currently hold the highest all-time NBA regular season win-loss record percentage. And then, of course, there's the Dallas Mavericks, the Houston Rockets, the WNBA's Dallas Wings, the NHL's Dallas Stars, the MLS's FC Dallas and Houston Dynamo, and the new kids on the block, Major League Rugby squads, including the Houston Sabercats, Dallas Jackals, and Austin Gilgronis.

### INTREPID TEXAN

More than 4,000 roller derby clubs can be found across America, and Austin has its own league. Dubbed the Texas Rollergirls, they compete at the Blood Shed, and the participating teams include the Texecutioners, Texas Chainsaws, Hell Marys, Hot Rod Honeys, and others.

texasrollergirls.org

Texas Rollergirls
Photo courtesy of Felicia Graham

# CREATE GRAFFITI
## AT THE CADILLAC RANCH

Amarillo's Cadillac Ranch, a row of 10 used Cadillacs buried nose-first in the ground at an angle that corresponds to the Great Pyramid in Giza (Egypt), was created by the Ant Farm, an avante-garde, hippie-freak architecture collective. Founded in San Francisco in the late 1960s, the Ant Farm got busy in the early 1970s, creating inexpensive, portable, vinyl shelters known as inflatables for progressive forums and communal "happenings." Their first happening in Texas was the 1972 construction of the futuristic House of the Century near Angleton. It was damaged by floods in the mid-1980s and now sits dilapidated. The world famous Cadillac Ranch was completed in 1974 with the assistance of eccentric Amarillo artist Stanley Marsh 3. The Cadillac Ranch probably says something subversive about the iconic Cadillac and American pop culture, but most folks just spray paint on a Caddy or two (there's a Home Depot right down the road) and take pictures.

Which is your cue, graffiti or no.

13651 I-40 Frontage Rd., Amarillo, TX 79124

### INTREPID TEXAN

On I-27 heading south out of Amarillo, you'll find an art installation backed by Stanley Marsh: two gigantic legs jutting vertically from a concrete base, known as "Ozymandias on the Plains."

Cadillac Ranch
Photo courtesy of Bob Protus

# SAY HELLO
## TO A RIVER

Late in the Texas literary classic *Goodbye to a River*, Fort Worth native John Graves becomes grave. "We will nearly be finished, I think, when we stop understanding the old pull toward green things and living things, toward dirt and rain and heat and what they spawn." The greenest, living, flowing things in Texas are rivers, and there are few things more Texan than floating a river. Canoes, kayaks, inner tubes, and inflatable vinyl tubes are available for purchase or rent at most river float destinations. Heck, today you can even put your hands on deluxe, two-passenger inflatable tubes (in any color), a tow-along tube for your ice cooler, and electric tube inflators. Whatever the vessel, river running or floating still stems from an "old pull toward green things" and a reverence for the arteries that carry life blood though the Lone Star state's most verdant and arid locales.

### INTREPID TEXAN

One of John Graves's canoe paddles can be found in the Wittliff Collections at Texas State University. thewittliffcollections.txstate.edu/collections/southwestern-writers.html

**Guadalupe River (Guadalupe River State Park)**
Practically a Texas pilgrimage.

3350 Park Rd. 31, Spring Branch, TX 78070
tpwd.texas.gov/state-parks/guadalupe-river

**San Marcos River**
Runs through the Texas State University campus; put in at Sewell Park.

601 University Dr., San Marcos, TX 78666
www.campusrecreation.txst.edu/places-to-go/outdoorcenter.html

**South Llano River (South Llano River State Park)**
A great ¾-mile stretch lies in the South Llano River State Park, but you can put in at one or two bridges farther down U.S. Hwy. 377 and make a day of it.

South Llano River State Park
1927 Park Rd. 73, Junction, TX 76849
tpwd.texas.gov/state-parks/south-llano-river

**Frio River (Garner State Park)**
Almost three prime miles of the Frio meander through Garner State Park.

234 RR 1050, Concan, TX 78838
tpwd.texas.gov/state-parks/garner

**Brazos River**
Put in at Rochelle's Canoe and Kayak Rental (southwest of Graford) or Hillbilly Haven Campground (right off I-20).

rochellescanoeandkayakrental.com
tubingthebrazos.com

# FEEL THE NEED
## FOR SPEED

Anybody who's seen *Ford v Ferrari* probably has some idea of who Carroll Shelby was, but few folks know he was born in Leesburg, Texas. From humble beginnings, Shelby became a championship racecar driver, a legendary racecar designer, and the chief progenitor of the Ford Motor Company's Cobra Mustang. But discussing Shelby just scratches the surface of Texas motorsports. Houston native A. J. Foyt is the only auto racer ever to win the Daytona 500, the Indy 500, the Rolex 24 at Daytona, and the 24 Hours of Le Mans. And he also netted seven wins in NASCAR. But the pantheon of Texas motorsports legends also includes Bobby and Terry Labonte of Corpus Christi, Johnny Rutherford of Fort Worth, and Bobby Hillin Jr. of Midland. So it's no surprise Texas is home to some impressive racecar tracks, including Texas Motor Speedway (Fort Worth), Devil's Bowl Speedway (Mesquite), Heart O' Texas Speedway (Elm Mott), and the Texas Motorplex for quarter-mile drag racing (Ennis).

texasmotorspeedway.com
devilsbowl.com
heartotexasspeedway.com
texasmotorplex.com

17

# GET MODERN
## IN FORT WORTH

The 12th-largest city in the United States, Cowtown (as it's also known) is the cowboy-est of all major American cities, but the big ranchers who drove the growth of the community aspired to a degree of sophistication as well. In the short term, these aspirations manifested themselves in parlor room pianos and a market for piano vendors. In the long term, they fostered a piano virtuoso named Van Cliburn, which led to Fort Worth becoming host of one of the most prestigious classical music events in the world, the quadrennial Van Cliburn International Piano Competition.

Early businesspeople followed the ranchers' lead, and today Fort Worth is home to three museums that make it an international art mecca of the first order. The Kimbell Art Museum sits in what is considered one of the state's foremost works of modern architecture and makes the itinerary for any serious art buff. The permanent collection features works from Rembrandt, Monet, and Picasso. The Amon Carter Museum of American Art houses one of the world's best collections of American art, including works by Winslow Homer, Edward Hopper, and Frederic Remington. The Modern Art Museum holds one of the most important collections of modern and contemporary art in the United States, displaying works from Picasso, Warhol, Jackson Pollock, and Francis Bacon. And all three museums are within one square mile of one another.

kimbellart.org, cartermuseum.org,
themodern.org

18

# TRACK
## A TEXAS MONSTER

For the chronically uninformed or tragically uninitiated, a Texas hero once played a huge role in a major monster slayin'. He was simply lost on the cutting room floor. His name was Quincey P. Morris, and he died after thrusting his Bowie knife into the heart of the namesake bloodsucker of Bram Stoker's 1897 horror classic, *Dracula*. When the first major movie version (featuring Bela Lugosi in his most iconic role) hit the silver screen, Morris was missing, and a bona fide Lone Star monster-slayer was consigned to oblivion. But Transylvania isn't the only monster haunt in the Western hemisphere or Morris's home state.

### INTREPID TEXAN

Two miles north of Saratoga off FM 787 lies the Scenic Saratoga Ghost Road where mystery lights have appeared repeatedly over the years. This former railroad bed is now eight miles of dirt road that takes a half hour to traverse in daylight. At night, however . . .

**Lake Worth Monster**

In June 1969, a "fishy man-goat" took up residence at Greer Island (now part of the Fort Worth Nature Center and Refuge), terrified locals, tossed tires at local police, and dominated the headlines until American astronauts landed on the moon. Some say the crafty whatsit still roams the area, mostly giving kids at Camp Carter insomnia.

**Bigfoot**

This smelly, lumbering Lone Star Wookiee and avid beef jerky enthusiast is said to ply the Big Thicket, the banks of Boggy Creek and stretches of the Piney Woods in far East Texas. Fool around and find out or play it safe like the rest of us. Hang your foodstuff in a tree 50 yards from your tent when you camp or post "bigfoot crossing" signs at your house to intrigue or annoy your neighbors.

**El Chupacabra**

The name of this recently resurgent creature translates from Spanish to "goat-sucker." It reportedly preys on livestock and pets, and its territory seems to range from southwest Texas to the Lone Star borderlands. Humbugs believe El Chupacabra is just a coyote with mange, but some folks think the creature is a strange, natural denizen of the region. Others claim it is a supernatural entity. You won't know if you don't go.

**La Lechuza**

The legends of La Lechuza spring from centuries-old Tex-Mex folklore. La Lechuza—which translates from Spanish to "owl" —was supposedly a witch who was caught practicing black magic and executed for her transgressions. Some say she came back as a large bird with a woman's face and goes swoop in the night to dispatch unsuspecting Texans. Others claim La Lechuza is a shapeshifter who exists as an ordinary witch during the day and transforms into a lady-faced bird of prey come sundown. (Not to be confused with la lechuga, which is Spanish for your garden variety head of lettuce.)

19

# CATCH A MOVIE
## AT A CLASSIC TEXAS THEATER

When you're not out chasing monsters, you can always glean tips for the process from the latest flicks playing at legendary Lone Star picture shows. There are a dozen films about El Chupacabra (including *Chupacabra vs. the Alamo*) and dozens more about Bigfoot (including the recent *The Man Who Killed Hitler and Bigfoot*—starring Sam Elliott). Or you can just sit back and enjoy the latest big-screen offerings in movie houses that were real magic in the age before VCRs, DVDs, Netflix, and the internet in general. Filmdom's mainstays are not extinct, and the proprietors and cinefiles who support them give the experience a human face and keep the silver screen alive and thriving.

### INTREPID TEXAN

Larry McMurtry's Booked Up bookstore is now closed, and Archer City's old Plaza Theatre is partially collapsed—but it was immortalized in *The Last Picture Show* in 1970 and, if you listen real close, you can still hear Ben Johnson's worldly chuckle.

**Texas Theatre (Dallas)**

Dating back to 1931, the Texas Theatre only plays classic movies and is best known for an offscreen drama: Lee Harvey Oswald was arrested for the murder of Police Officer J. D. Tippit here on November 22, 1963. The Oak Cliff Foundation purchased the theater in 2001, and it was added to the National Register of Historic Places a couple of years later. It's had major upgrades since, but it sticks to the recent and not-so-recent oldies.

231 W Jefferson Blvd., Dallas, TX 75208
(214) 948-1546, thetexastheatre.com

**Paramount Theater (Abilene)**

An Abilene treasure dating back to 1930 and featuring Spanish Colonial Revival decor, the main theater also only features classic movies. The venue was designed to look like a courtyard at night, and the ceiling features a night sky and stars behind projected clouds.

352 Cypress St., Abilene, TX 79601
(325) 676-9620, www.paramountabilene.com

**Stars & Stripes Drive-In Theatre (Lubbock)**

Featuring new double features all year round, Stars and Stripes opened in 2003, but features one of the best sunset views in Texas as well as Rockin' Eats and Tasty Treats at its 50's Café. Get there half an hour to an hour early to take in a West Texas sunset. Stars & Stripes is the home of the Ay Chihuahua Original Mexican Sandwich.

5101 Clovis Hwy., Lubbock, TX 79416
(806) 749-7469, driveinusa.com/lubbock/

**Big Sky Drive-In Theatre (Midland)**

This pet-friendly, al fresco cinema offers three double features nightly, plus a Lone Star-sized concessions menu. Grab Fido and/or the kiddos and take in the big sky before the big screens light up.

6200 W Hwy. 80, Midland, TX 79706
(432) 617-3001, www.bigskytheatre.com

General Ignacio Zaragoza
Photo courtesy of Colección Museo de Historia Mexicana

# CELEBRATE
## CINCO DE MAYO

Often mistaken for Mexico's Independence Day, Cinco de Mayo actually celebrates the Mexican army's unlikely defeat of the sneaky French at the Battle of Puebla on May 5, 1862.

While Texans and Americans were embroiled in the Civil War, Napoleon III decided to establish a French Empire in Mexico. A large French force landed at Veracruz and vanquished it relatively easily. Then, when they began marching inland toward Mexico City, an unofficial, quasi-Texan intervened. The vastly outnumbered Mexican forces were led by Ignacio Zaragoza, a general and politician who was born in 1829 in a Mexican community that later became known as Goliad (in the Republic and state of Texas). As soil hardly knows the difference, Zaragoza is a Tex-Mex hero at the very least, and we should laud his historic victory. Without it, we might be addicted to Tex-Franco or Franco-Tex instead of Tex-Mex.

So drink some Dos Equis (or Negra Modelo, Tecate, Pacifico, or Corona), grab some tacos, attend one of the parades, and celebrate one of our heroes.

### INTREPID TEXAN

A bronze statue of Ignacio Zaragoza is located adjacent to Presidio La Bahía in the Goliad State Park and Historic Site.

108 Park Rd 6, Goliad, TX 77963
(361) 645-3405, tpwd.texas.gov/state-parks/goliad

# TAKE A FRIEND TO TRY
## THE 72-OUNCE BIG TEXAN CHALLENGE

Aspiring gorgers have one hour to consume this massive beef bomb and all the fixins, which include a shrimp cocktail, a baked potato, a salad, and a roll. The $72 cost of the meal must be paid up front, and that amount is refunded if the challenge is completed. Don't expect a reenactment of the boiled egg scene from *Cool Hand Luke* because all takers have to cut the steak themselves and feed themselves. Once an attempt has started, ambitious eaters can't get up or leave the table. If a participant can consume the entire meal in 60 minutes or less, they emerge victorious and are immortalized forever in the coveted Big Texan 72 oz Hall of Fame. But biter beware: as of the writing of this book, 87,655 dietary daredevils had attempted this feat, and only 10,077 had gulped victorious.

7701 Interstate 40 East Access Rd., Amarillo, TX 79118
(806) 372-6000, bigtexan.com/72-oz-steak

22

# VISIT
## A COUNTY SEAT

Once known for its seven curative springs, Lampasas now boasts the world's largest spur (35-feet tall and weighing 10,000 lbs.) and the refreshing Hancock Springs Pool. Gainesville is the birthplace of the world's first "fastest man" (Charley Paddock) and now hosts America's only annual Medal of Honor Program every April, inviting surviving armed forces Congressional Medal of Honor recipients to participate in a motorcade, parade, dinner, banquet, and more, all expenses paid! Fort Stockton boasts the state's largest Roadrunner (Paisano Pete) and stages a Water Carnival every summer, featuring theatrical pool performances, synchronized swimming, and water dancing! Goliad is the birthplace of Cinco de Mayo hero Ignacio Zaragoza and a massive, fascinating hanging tree. Nacogdoches is the oldest city in Texas and the current home of the legendary Texas Mojo Storyteller Joe R. Lansdale! Corsicana now calls itself "the state's greatest detour," and Palestine, which used to be the fourth-largest city in Texas, is preparing for a comeback! There are 254 counties in the Lone Star state, and they all feature fun to be had, history to learn, and yarns to unravel. Learn it, know it, live it.

# MOSEY UP TO THE BAR
## IN A TEXAS SALOON

A Texan may not have invented beer drinking or bars, but Texans have perfected the former and ardently support the latter. Texas is, after all, home to Shiner Bock, Pearl Beer, Rahr & Sons, and too many new craft beers to name, and the state even has a beer named after it: Lone Star.

Texans have also been known to imbibe lugubrious amounts of tequila, which you'd think we invented (especially considering the massive quantities of it consumed herein), and margaritas, which some cocktail historians maintain was invented here in 1948 at the Balinese Room in Galveston.

A good way to tell when a Texan has had too much to drink? When he or she is drinking out of his or her own boot.

### INTREPID TEXAN

Located in the upscale Joule Hotel in downtown Dallas, the Midnight Rambler is a subterranean, craft cocktail lounge you'd expect to find in a posh NYC hotel. Descend the stairs, ignore the stares, and imbibe the highfalutin libations.

1530 Main St., Dallas, TX 75201
(214) 261-4601, midnightramblerbar.com

**Menger Hotel Bar (San Antonio)**
One of the Top 10 most historic bars in the United States.

300 E Crockett St., San Antonio, TX 78205
(210) 223-4361, www.mengerhotel.com

**White Elephant Saloon (Fort Worth)**
The site of high-stakes poker games and several gunfights in the early days and still a Cowtown favorite.

106 E. Exchange Ave., Fort Worth, TX 76164
(817) 624-8273, whiteelephantsaloon.com

**Devil's Backbone Tavern (San Marcos area)**
Immortalized by alt-folk singer-songwriter Todd Snider in "The Story of the Ballad of the Devil's Backbone Tavern."

4041 Farm to Market 32, Fischer, TX 78623
(830) 964-2544, www.devilsbackbonetavern.com

**11th Street Cowboy Bar (Bandera)**
The biggest little bar in Texas and bras hang from the ceiling.

307 11th St., Bandera, TX 78003
(830) 796-4849, www.11thstreetcowboybar.com

**Lone Star Saloon (Houston)**
Open since 1955, a place with attitude and latitude. Sits in the heart of downtown Houston, just blocks away from the Greyhound station.

1900 Travis, Houston, TX 77002
(713) 757-1616

# GET LONE STAR LITERARY

Though American novelist, poet, short-story writer, art critic, and literary critic John Updike was born in Reading, Pennsylvania, I'm ready to lead an effort to make him an honorary Texan. Yes, he received a Pulitzer Prize for Fiction and a National Book Award for Fiction, but, no, I'm not sure he ever wrote anything about the Lone Star state—except this (which could have been written about any community in any state): "Bookstores are lonely forts, spilling light onto the sidewalk. They civilize their neighborhoods."

Larry McMurtry, Katherine Anne Porter, John Graves, Joe R. Lansdale, Cormac McCarthy, Molly Ivins, Elmer Kelton, William Goyen, William Humphrey, Carmen Tafolla, Beverly Lowry, Elizabeth Crook, Stephen Graham Jones, and so many others from here and from everywhere—visit a lonely fort. Bask in their light.

### INTREPID TEXAN

The Twig Book Shop is located in the fabulous Pearl neighborhood of San Antonio. Books, brunch, shopping—it's one of the best places to be in Texas on a Saturday!

306 Pearl Pkwy, Unit 106, San Antonio, TX 78215
(210) 826-6411

**Book People (Austin)**
603 N. Lamar Blvd., Austin, TX 78703
(512) 472-5050, bookpeople.com

**Gladewater Books**
109 E. Pacific Ave., Gladewater, TX 75647
(903) 845-4843

**Literarity Book Shop (El Paso)**
5411 N. Mesa St., El Paso, TX 79912
(915) 307-4760

**Front Street Books (Alpine)**
121 E. Holland Ave., Alpine, TX 79830
(432) 837-3360, frontstreetbooks.com

**Recycled Books (Denton)**
200 N. Locust St., Denton, TX 76201
(940) 566-5688, recycledbooks.com

**Brazos Books (Houston)**
2421 Bissonnet St., Houston, TX 77005
(713) 523-0701, brazosbookstore.com

**Galveston Bookshop (Galveston)**
317 23rd St., Galveston, TX 77550
(409) 750-8200, galvestonbookshop.com

**Interabang Books (Dallas)**
5600 W Lovers Ln., Ste. 142, Dallas, TX 75209
(214) 484-4289, interabangbooks.com

25

# WATCH
## A WRASSLIN' MATCH

In the *Bleacher Report*'s list of the "Greatest Wrestling Families of All Time," the first two slots are occupied by the Dallas-area Von Erichs and the Funks of the infamous "Double Cross Ranch" near Amarillo. Patriarchs Fritz Von Erich and Dory Funk were both savvy wrestling promoters in terms of business acumen and promising progeny, and the Von Erich's are still producing wrestling superstars three generations in. There's hardly a boy who grew up in Texas in the latter half of the 20th century who didn't at least "Indian" or arm wrestle, and a few of the bigger, tougher ones went on to steer wrestle. And before you give the idea of seeing a wrestling match the high hat, remember that legendary Gonzo journalist and author Hunter S. Thompson got his start on a professional wrestling beat. And professional wrestling is also the best metaphor for Texas politics.

**Top of Texas Pro Wrestling (Amarillo)**
Professional Wrestling back in the Texas Panhandle.

2650 Dumas Dr., Amarillo, TX 79107
(806) 382-3839, topoftexasprofessionalwrestling.com

**Houston Premier Arena**
Plenty of true belivers left in H-Town.

7122 Avenue B, Houston, TX 77011
(832) 380-1979

**Dickies Arena**
Hosts WWE Smackdown Events on occasion.

1911 Montgomery St., Fort Worth, TX 76107
(817) 402-9000, dickiesarena.com

**Metroplex Wrestling (Bedford)**
Every Saturday night.

510 Harwood Rd., Ste. D, Bedford, TX 76021
metroplex-wrestling.square.site

**American Airlines Center**
Holds WWE events, etc.

2500 Victory Park Ln., Dallas, TX 75219
(214) 665-4299, americanairlinescenter.com

Guadalupe Mountains National Park
Photo courtesy of Jay Gannett

# PARKS AND RECREATION

# EXPERIENCE
## A BIG BEND STATE OF MIND

More than any other park, site, place, or activity, the Big Bend echoes a popular Texas mantra. It's a state of mind. The roads widen, and the days stretch out. Time expands, and it's impossible to get anywhere fast. The Big Bend National Park is as big as the entire state of Rhode Island, and a three- or four-day visit hardly scratches the surface.

Protecting more than 1,000 species of flora, at least 450 species of birds, 56 species of reptiles, and 75 species of mammals, this 801,163-acre spread is a national park system rock star. Mountains, desert, forest, river, hot springs, dinosaur bones, fossilized sea creatures, volcanic dykes, black bear, mountain lions, hiking, biking, canoeing, kayaking, camping on high ground, camping on low ground—you really can't get your head around it until you've been there—and once you've been there, you can't stop going back.

The 13-mile South Rim Trail is one of the best hikes in world, but the tough Emory Peak Trail, the picturesque Lost Mine Trail, the Boquillas Canyon Trail (down to the Rio), the dramatic Santa Elena Trail, the stark Ernest Tinaja hike, and even the kooky Grapevine Hills jaunt are all sublime. The easy Hot Springs hike near the Rio Grande Village is always in order after one of the longer treks (remember to bring a towel).

The drives are equally impressive, and you can also book overnight canoe or kayak excursions through Santa Elena Canyon. The park-maintained campsites in the Chisos Basin and the primitive campsites scattered throughout the terrain can be reserved, and if you plan far enough ahead, you can get good, air-conditioned accommodations at the Chisos Mountains Lodge.

Don't put this off. The Big Bend National Park is big and intimidating, but around these parts, it's a peerless landscape for the adventurous.

nps.gov/bibe
chisosmountainslodge.com

## INTREPID TEXAN

Tex-Mex and BBQ may be the heavy hitters in terms of the Lone Star palate—but don't say that in front of chili folks. Chili is a formidable Texas dish in its own right and makes a good case for a Lone Star culinary trifecta, especially since our big chili cook-off earns much more acclaim than our BBQ contests. In fact, the Terlingua Chili Cook-off is actually two chili cook-offs held in the same town at the same time. The Original Terlingua International Championship Chili Cook Off and the Chili Appreciation Society International's Texas International Chili Championship commence simultaneously in late October and end in early November. Both events offer chili options galore and bring in musical acts for entertainment.

abowlofred.com

27

# HIKE
## THE GUADALUPE MOUNTAINS NATIONAL PARK

The Guadalupe Mountains aren't as tall as the Himalayas, the Andes, or even the Rockies, but—with all due respect to my Hindu, Andean, and Coloradan friends—they're in Texas, so they hold their own and then some. Few views are as majestic as the Guadalupe Mountains approached on a clear day from the west or staring out once atop the 8,751-foot Guadalupe Peak. From the west, you encounter the Guadalupe Mountains as a sky island towering above a flat, white sand salt basin. From the Peak itself, you see hundreds of miles of the Chichuahuan Desert in every direction. If the strenuous 8.4-mile round-trip hike to the peak doesn't fit into your plans, a quick half-mile jaunt into the western Salt Basin is fun, or you can visit the Pine Springs Visitor Center for information on other excursions, including the excellent (moderate) 6.8-mile round trip McKittrick Springs Trail (the Springs being the only place in Texas where trout still run naturally) and the picturesque Devil's Hall.

The Guadalupe Mountains were sacred to the Apache, and some reportedly snuck back and remained after their official confinement to reservations. Rumors persist that their campsites and tepees were stumbled upon by visitors well into the early 20th century.

You can find some excellent picnic spots on the way up to the Visitors Center, some good developed campsites once there, and, of course, primitive camping on the interior. It's been a hundred years since the last reliable Apache sighting, but don't wait. This is another experience that shouldn't be postponed.

Pine Springs Visitor Center
400 Pine Canyon Dr., Salt Flat, TX 79847
(915) 828-3251, nps.gov/gumo/index.htm

## INTREPID TEXAN

When you're heading up US Highway 62/180 to get to the Pine Springs Visitor Center (Headquarters), watch for a Guadalupe Canyon sign. You'll see a gate on the north side of the road with turnstiles. It's old, abandoned US 180, and you can hike up it for 500 yards or so—but watch your step. Nature is reclaiming the road.

# GET LOST
## ON CADDO LAKE

Just kidding. Because people do it every weekend.

Too many Texans (and Americans) view lakes simply as bodies of water created for perfecting their water sports acumen (including but not limited to waterskiing, wakeboarding, and jet skiing), and Caddo Lake is anathema to said mindset. The snaking, meandering 26,000-acre Caddo Lake is like a primordial soup, in places densely forested, but everywhere teeming with life and thick with mystery. Legendary Eagles recording artist Don Henley was born in East Texas and has a property on Caddo. He says, "If there's any evidence of divinity on this Earth at all, it certainly exists here."

A significant number of ambitious landlubbers venture out onto the lake in canoes and kayaks during the daytime but find themselves lost as nightfall arrives. They wind up stuck out there overnight, feasted on by mosquitoes and terrorized by howls of Bigfoot or whatever other creatures that prowl the Caddo after hours. If you're paddling out very far, play it safe and hire a guide.

### INTREPID TEXAN

The Piney Woods–nestled Caddo Lake State Park offers good fishing opportunities and excellent camping and cabin accomodations.
tpwd.texas.gov/state-parks/caddo-lake

29

# VISIT
## PALO DURO CANYON

Anyone who has spent much time around Texans knows they usually don't cotton to playing second, much less third, fiddle, but Mexico's Copper Canyon is the deepest and widest canyon in North America, and the Grand Canyon is the deepest and largest in the United States. Our Palo Duro Canyon is third to the former and second to the latter but no less spectacular. Approximately 120 miles long and several miles wide in places, Palo Duro has depths of up to 1,200 feet. In the Palo Duro Canyon State Park, the highlights include 30 miles of hiking and horseback trails, the popular Lighthouse Peak rock formation, and striated canyon walls (highlighted with bright reds, yellows, and oranges). Artist Georgia O'Keeffe lived in the area in the early 20th century and made use of Palo Duro as a subject, describing it as "a burning, seething cauldron, filled with dramatic light and color."

Palo Duro Canyon State Park
11450 State Hwy. Park Rd. 5, Canyon, TX 79015
(806) 488-2227, tpwd.texas.gov/state-parks/palo-duro-canyon

### INTREPID TEXAN

The Texas Parks and Wildlife Department rents three cabins built by the Civilian Conservation Corps on the Palo Duro Canyon rim, and they cannot be recommended highly enough in terms of location and views.

# BEACHCOMB
## PADRE ISLAND NATIONAL SEASHORE

The longest undeveloped stretch of public beach in the continental United States (60 miles) and part of the longest undeveloped barrier island in the world, the 130,434-acre Padre Island National Seashore is a national treasure. Though plenty of beach lovers are always there, they congregate at the 5-mile and 10-mile marker points, camping, picnicking, sunbathing, swimming, bodysurfing, and shell hunting. The crowd gets scarce out past the 15- and 20-mile markers, and by the 25-mile marker, you can have a wide swathe of beach to yourself. A four-wheel-drive vehicle is recommended out past the 5-mile marker, and any food, drink, or camping gear you require you'll have to bring along. The weekly fee for this primitive stretch of paradise is affordable. If your old VW van will still start, you can even buy a yearlong stay!

Starting around the 15-mile marker, critically endangered Kemp's ridley sea turtles come up the beach and nest. A local, all-volunteer turtle patrol keeps a watchful eye and later makes sure the hatchlings make it out to sea.

The Padre Island National Seashore is a Lone Star wonder replete with fascination, mystery, and discovery. For instance, after the SS *Marine Sulphur Queen* set sail from Beaumont in

1963 and disappeared in the Bermuda Triangle, a message in a bottle (apparently from one of its crew) washed up on the Seashore two months later.

If you venture out just past the 50-mile marker at low tide, you can still spot the bulkhead of the SS *Nicaragua* about a hundred feet out. The 190-foot steamer ran ashore in 1912, and locals visited the wreck in their Model Ts for years afterward.

Keep your eyes peeled and your sunblock thick. Somebody may need help.

Malakite Visitor Center
20420 Park Road 22, Corpus Christi, TX 78418
nps.gov/pais/planyourvisit/visitorcenter.htm

### INTREPID TEXAN

Once a year every year since 1995, the Friends of Padre have organized a Big Shell Beach Cleanup in the Big Shell portion of the Padre Island National Seashore, enlisting 12,925 volunteers altogether and removing 3,122,000 pounds of trash from this remote and wild stretch of 4-Wheel Drive Only beach. Helping or chipping in would be a noble hoot.
friendsofpadre.com

31

# DIVE INTO
## A TEXAS SWIMMING HOLE

Texas was recently called the swimming hole capital of the United States, and everyone around the country was surprised except those who live here. In a place that stays as hot as Texas, every swimming hole offers an indispensable oasis where folks who are tough enough to stand the heat can let their hair down and rejuvenate. In extreme cases, these reprieves are granted in the form of water troughs or stock tanks, but the best options are rivers, lakes, and spring-fed pools. Most of the top spots are in Central Texas, but you can also find a few refreshing standouts in East and West Texas.

The rest is simple. Jump in, cool off, and repeat as necessary.

**San Solomon Springs (Balmorhea Springs State Park)**

The best swimming hole in Texas, perhaps uniquely awesome because it requires planning and a serious jaunt to enjoy. It is strongly recommended that you purchase day passes in advance for the summer months, weekends, school breaks, and holidays. They often sell out for the summer months.

9207 TX-17, Toyahvale, TX 79786

(432) 375-2370, tpwd.texas.gov/state-parks/balmorhea

**Devil's Waterhole (Inks Lake State Park)**

A refreshing pool between pink granite cliffs, perfect for swimming and cliff diving.

3630 Park Rd. 4 West, Burnet, TX 78611

(512) 793-2223, tpwd.texas.gov/state-parks/inks-lake

**Blanco River (Blanco State Park)**

Another refreshing, spring-fed waterway.

101 Park Road 23, Blanco, TX 78606

(830) 833-4333, tpwd.texas.gov/state-parks/blanco

**Hamilton Pool Preserve**

Incredible natural grotto pool; call ahead for reservations.

24300 Hamilton Pool Rd., Dripping Springs, TX 78620

(512) 264-2740, parks.traviscountytx.gov/find-a-park/hamilton-pool

**Krause Springs**

On a 115-acre property that has 32 springs, a man-made pool, and a natural pool.

424 County Road 404, Spicewood, TX 78669

(401) 236-7554, krausesprings.net

**Tyler Lake (Tyler State Park)**

The diving raft is great place for escaping the heat in the Piney Woods.

789 Park Rd. 16, Tyler, TX 75706

(903) 597-5338, tpwd.texas.gov/state-parks/tyler

# CLIMB
## ENCHANTED ROCK

A Lone Star version of Australia's Ayer's Rock, the Hill Country's Enchanted Rock has enchanted locals and visitors for 12,000 years. In the daytime, the pink granite batholith, which sits in the 1,643-acre Enchanted Rock State Natural Area, rises from the surrounding landscape somewhat unobtrusively, a subtle vertical anomaly; but at night, it's known to groan and crackle as it cools down, converting humbugs and naysayers with equal aplomb.

A good, short jaunt for regular hikers and a great, slow slog for less seasoned outdoors partakers, the Summit Trail ascends 40 stories in a little over a half-mile, and when you arrive up high, you're treated with a terrific view and some perfect backdrop boulders. After you catch your breath, check out the Enchanted Rock Cave and Lunch Rock.

Enchanted Rock State Natural Area
16710 Ranch Road 965, Fredericksburg, TX 78624
(830) 685-3636, tpwd.texas.gov/state-parks/enchanted-rock

### INTREPID TEXAN

The informative National Museum of the Pacific War is only 18 miles south on Ranch Road 965 in Fredericksburg, the hometown of Chester W. Nimitz, Commander in Chief of the U.S. Pacific Fleet in World War II.
311 E. Austin St., Fredericksburg, TX 78624
(830) 997-8600, pacificwarmuseum.org

# CATCH A DUNE
## AT THE MONAHANS SANDHILLS

Ever surf a sand dune? You can at the Monahans Sandhills State Park.

Located halfway between Odessa and Pecos, this 3,800-acre gem is home to thousands of dunes, some over 70 feet in height. The park headquarters rents sand-surfing disks and offers interpretive exhibits. The park itself has several picnic spots and more than two dozen camp sites featuring the standard amenities.

The Monahans Sandhills are a great stop on any long trek across West Texas, but make sure you bring flip-flops and sunscreen.

To reach the park, travel Interstate 20
and exit mile marker 86 to Park Road 41
(432) 557-3479, tpwd.texas.gov/state-parks/monahans-sandhills

### INTREPID TEXAN

Wander a hundred yards into the Monahans Sandhills, and you can pretend you're Lawrence of Arabia. Drive 38 miles east on I-20, and you can envision yourself a Stone Age Druid in southwest England. A mind-blowing replica of Stonehenge sits on the campus of the University of Texas of the Permian Basin.

Preston Smith Rd., Odessa, TX 79762
(432) 552-2806

# EXPLORE
## A TEXAS CAVERN

"The very cave you are afraid to enter turns out to be the source of what you are looking for." Influential American author Joseph Campbell said that, and he was really on to (or into) something. Texas caverns are an underutilized resource in terms of what many adventuresome souls are looking for, namely, inspiring recreation and once-in-a-lifetime experiences. You can, of course, take the basic tours and spend an hour following a guide on a lighted, leisurely pathway ticking off the prescribed sights. There's nothing wrong with it, especially if you're too young, too old, or limited by health conditions; but if you aren't too young, too old, or physically limited, you should tackle some of the "Wild" or "Adventure" cave tours. Squeeze through narrow passages, cross low-ceiling stretches of limestone on your hands and knees, get a little scraped up and muddy—but don't hit, bump, or dislodge your head lamp. It gets awfully dark down there.

**Longhorn Cavern State Park**
Right down the road from Inks Lake State Park; the two make a great summer day combination.

6211 Park Road 4 South, Burnet, TX 78611
(512) 715-9000, visitlonghorncavern.com

**Caverns of Sonora**
Check out the helictites, and repel down a cavern chamber wall.

1711 Pvt Rd. 4468, Sonora, TX 76950
(325) 387-3105, cavernsofsonora.com

**Kickapoo Cavern State Park**
Primitive tours are available every Saturday, but reservations are required.

20939 Ranch to Market Road 674, Brackettville, TX 78832
(830) 563-2342, tpwd.texas.gov/state-parks/kickapoo-cavern

**Inner Space Cavern**
Accidentally discovered by the Texas Highway Department in 1963 during the construction of Interstate 35; one of the best preserved caves in Texas.

4200 N. Interstate 35 Frontage Rd., Georgetown, TX 78626
(512) 931-2283, innerspacecavern.com

**Natural Bridge Caverns**
One of the largest cave complexes in the state; the "Watchtower" and the "Castle of White Giants" steal the show.

26495 Natural Bridge Caverns Rd., San Antonio, TX 78266
(210) 651-6101, naturalbridgecaverns.com

**Cave with No Name**
Many say the this unnamed treasure is the most beautiful cave in Texas.

325 Kreutzberg Rd., Boerne, TX 78006
(830) 537-4212, cavewithoutaname.com

35

# DISAPPEAR
## IN THE DEVIL'S RIVER STATE NATURAL AREA

Forty-five miles from Del Rio and 80 miles from anywhere else, the most devilish aspect of the Devil's River these days is getting to it. Once you spot the sign on the west side of U.S. Hwy. 277, you take a 25-mile gravel road to the State Natural Area office, sign in, park a few miles farther down, and then hike a shadeless near mile to the river. At the end of the hike, you'll be tempted to jump in the river at the base of the last hill, but take a hard right instead and go another quarter-mile or so farther. There the water winds along the limestone banks in Caribbean hues.

Most Texans never visit the Devil's River State Natural Area, and that's a shame—but perhaps better for the hardy spirits who do. They have a spring-fed oasis to themselves, and less traffic means a better chance for the threatened species that live in the Devil's River Watershed to survive and thrive.

21715 Dolan Creek Rd., Del Rio, TX 78840
(830) 395-2133, tpwd.texas.gov/state-parks/devils-river

### INTREPID TEXAN

Cocky Confederate General John Bell Hood's mettle was first tested in the Battle of Devil's River in 1857. He didn't apply the lessons he learned going forward.

36

# DISCOVER
## THE DEVIL'S SINKHOLE

Another neglected natural wonder in southwest Texas is the Devil's Sinkhole. When you first observe this sudden 50-foot-wide, 400-foot-deep opening in the Edwards Plateau, you think deer, stray horses, cattle, or other critters would have accidentally plunged to their deaths while in full flight when they encountered it, but the only victims seem to be rattlesnakes, which the fall doesn't always kill. Scientists have never discovered a larger animal bone in the Sinkhole, but that may be because of the permanent residents. The Sinkhole is home to several million Mexican free-tailed bats that emerge at sunset. The best time to see the bat show is from April through October.

The Devil's Sinkhole State Natural Area is a long way from the usual tourist attractions, but it's well worth a detour. The short hikes required to reach the site are conducted by the all-volunteer Devil's Sinkhole Society, which has an office in downtown Rocksprings.

Devil's Sinkhole Society
101 N. Sweeten St., Rocksprings, TX 78880
(830) 683-2287, tpwd.texas.gov/state-parks/devils-sinkhole

### INTREPID TEXAN

The Devil's Sinkhole was cordoned off and protected by marines in the early 1940s because the bats there were utilized for a secret weapon that competed with the Manhattan Project to end World War II. Ask your Sinkhole guide about Project X-Ray.

# GREET AUTUMN
## AT DAINGERFIELD STATE PARK

Texans have a special affinity for autumn. The cool late September breezes mean the furnace-like heat of summer has been turned off (or at least down), and the leaves will soon begin to take on bright colors. Daingerfield State Park may be the best place in the state to witness this transition.

By November, the dazzling fall foliage of the maple and sweetgum trees reaches its peak and offers a pleasant respite from whatever troubles you. The short hike around Lake Daingerfield is one of the most beautiful in the state and a great opportunity for quiet meditation.

The park also offers excellent picnicking, fishing, swimming, and a number of potluck Dutch oven events throughout the year. The park accommodations include 58 campsites with standard amenities and three vintage cabins built by the Civilian Conservation Corps.

455 Park Rd. 17, Daingerfield, TX 75638
(903) 645-292, tpwd.texas.gov/state-parks/daingerfield

### INTREPID TEXAN

The current holder of the national record for most shutouts in a season, the 1983 Daingerfield Tigers are considered the most dominant team in Texas football history and rank second only to the 1969 Texas Longhorns National Championship squad on the list of the most memorable gridiron squads at the professional, college, or high school level.

# PEDAL THROUGH
## A RAILROAD TUNNEL

The Caprock Canyon's Trailway extends 64 miles along abandoned railway beds and runs through three separate Panhandle counties. Opened in 1993, it features more than 50 bridges and a thrilling path through the 742-foot Clarity Tunnel, an old railroad passage through the Caprock.

The Caprock Canyons State Park is an excellent locale for hikes, mountain bikes, and horse rides but also compelling lessons in geology. The paved road in exposes visitors to 250 million years of geological formation punctuated by white streaks that cap the layer of each era. Paleo Indians hunted the ancestors of modern bison here for 10,000 years, and the 15,314-acre spread is currently home to the Official State Bison Herd. The herd is populated by descendants of Charles and Mary Ann Goodnight's successful 1878 attempt to save the species, which had dwindled from more than 30 million head to only a thousand when the Goodnights commenced the effort.

850 Caprock Canyon Park Rd., Quitaque, TX 79255
(806) 455-1492, tpwd.texas.gov/state-parks/caprock-canyons

### INTREPID TEXAN

Some of the most impressive canyon features in the Caprock region, namely the Narrows and Linguish Falls, lie on private land near Silverton.

39

# LAND
## THE ONE THAT GOT AWAY

My old friend Charles "Charlie" Roy Rogers is gone now, but his legend lingers on. One day while fishing the Brazos in a canoe, ol' Roy's eyelids grew heavy, and he decided to take a nap. He tossed the haydite block he used for an anchor overboard, but thought twice about leaving his fishing line out. He didn't want to lose it or the bait, so he cut the cast line, set the rod in the bottom of his canoe, and tied the line to a belt loop on his jeans. After an indeterminate period of napping, whatever got a hold of his bait jerked him out of the boat. "If I hadn't got those jeans off," he said, "I'd have drowned right there." Most Texas anglers have one of these stories, but Charlie's was a keeper. And it's never too late to avenge him.

**Choke Canyon Reservoir**

Located on the Frio River east of Three Rivers on State Highway 72, the Reservoir is a fishing tourney hotspot.

tpwd.texas.gov/fishboat/fish/recreational/lakes/choke_canyon/access.phtml

**Laguna Adventures Floating Cabin Rentals (Corpus Christi Bay/Laguna Madre)**

I spent a weekend there a few years back with a friend we called Dr. Fish. They're still cataloguing and classifying the creatures we pulled out of the water.

lagunaadventures.com/floating-cabin-rentals

**Lake O' the Pines**

Ample vegetation, largemouth bass, smallmouth bass, crappie, sunfish and channel, blue and flathead catfish. Did somebody say fish fry? Located on Big Cypress Creek in the Cypress River Basin, 25 miles northeast of Longview.

tpwd.texas.gov/fishboat/fish/recreational/lakes/lop

**Lake Texoma**

I'm not terribly religious, but when I think of this lake on the Oklahoma/Texas border, John 21:3 in the Bible comforts me: "Simon Peter saith unto them, I go a fishing. They say unto him, We also go with thee." The blue catfish in Texoma can get as big as Aggie linebackers, and I shudder to think about trying to boat one of these leviathans by myself.

tpwd.texas.gov/fishboat/fish/recreational/lakes/texoma

**Aquilla Lake**

A great little fishing hole in Hill County, 11 miles south of Hillsboro.

tpwd.texas.gov/fishboat/fish/recreational/lakes/aquilla

View of SpaceX's Starship SN8 prototype launch
from South Padre Island
Photo courtesy of Forest Katsch

# BASK IN THE SUN
## AT SOUTH PADRE ISLAND

The Spring Break capital of Texas and one of the most popular Spring Break destinations in the United States, South Padre Island is arguably a better place to visit before or after March when the college crowds recede and prices drop, and especially if you're looking for some peace and quiet.

South Padre Island was separated from the Padre Island National Seashore by the installation of the Mansfield Channel in 1964, and the first five miles or so north from the Queen Isabella Causeway offers accomodations in line with most all the standard amenities of modern beach resort meccas. The next 29 miles of the public beach stretch northerly and are more primitive.

At the base of the causeway, the Port Isabell Lighthouse is the only lighthouse in Texas that offers public access. Out in the Gulf itself, the number of watersports seem to increase every year. If the sun and sand are not enough, windsurfing, kiteboarding, kayaking, fishing, surf-fishing, or skydiving are all viable options.

sopadre.com

# SEE
## THE HUECO TANKS

The Hueco Tanks are a unique rock formation in the desert just northeast of El Paso. The "tanks" are actually hollows in the rocks that catch and hold rainwater, which makes them particularly indispensable for the animals that make the dry region their home. The site has been important to Native Americans in the area for more than 10,000 years, and the hike, which is fairly moderate, allows you to view some of the 5,000 pictographs they etched onto the rocks.

An excellent destination for rock climbing and bouldering as well, the park is never crowded, and the Tanks are a great way to spend a day away from El Paso or the Guadalupe Mountains (90 miles east on U.S. Hwy. 62). Camping sites are available inside the 860-acre park if you want to make a day of it.

Hueco Tanks State Historic Site
6900 Hueco Tanks Road No. 1, El Paso, TX 79938
(915) 857-1135, tpwd.texas.gov/state-parks/hueco-tanks

42

# BEND THE RULES
## AT COLORADO BEND

Colorado Bend State Park bends the rules. Some state parks have caves but very little water (inside or outside). Many state parks have waterways to play in, but no spelunking opportunities. Most state parks also offer water and/or electric options for camping. Colorado Bend State Park is like an adventure buffet for purists. For primitive campers only, it offers cave tours, a river, the fantastic, cascading Spicewood Springs, 14 miles of bike trails, an additional 16 miles of bike or hike trails, and the magnificent 65-foot Gorman Falls. Yes, you have to settle for compost toilets and back to nature digs, but still. It hardly seems fair.

tpwd.texas.gov/state-parks/colorado-bend

# PERFORM
## A TEXTREME FEAT

In the early summer of 1980, my father had a notion and he acted on it. He wanted to take his 10- and 12-year-old sons on an adventure. Not Six Flags or Putt-Putt or a day at the waterslides that were popping up—a real adventure. So that early June, we (and some friends) dipped three canoes in the Rio Grande at Boquillas Station at the Big Bend National Park and set out for Langtry. No cell phones, no GPS, and cots instead of tents. Eight days in and about 160 miles later, we were down to two canoes and had no food. We probably still could have made it, but a motorboat headed upstream gave us an assist. Textreme feats are not for the faint of heart or the impulsive. My dad was neither, and we were still lucky. But the impression the journey made on me was indelible.

Extreme adventures still abound in Texas, and I would be remiss if I didn't encourage folks to try at least one.

**Endure the Hotter'n Hell 100**

One of the oldest, largest, and least hospitable cycling events in the world, the Hotter'n Hell 100 is a Texas-sized dare, pitting wild-eyed fitness junkies against the sweltering furnace-like heat of a North Texas summer. In 1982, the Wichita Falls Bicycle Club chipped in with a crazy idea to promote their town's centennial celebration: 100 miles in 100-degree weather. Today, as the event's webpage notes, it's a "Texas 'Ride' of Passage."

Held annually on the last Saturday in August, the Hotter'n Hell 100 attracts more than 10,000 riders a year. The event begins at 7:05 a.m., and, as a precautionary measure, prospective 100-mile riders must reach the 60-mile mark no later than 12:30 p.m. If they don't make it, they do not qualify to finish the 100-mile segment and settle for the completion of a shorter route. Most participants finish the course in six to nine hours.

hh100.org

### Try the Texas Water Safari

Held annually the second Saturday in June since 1963, the Safari is a 262-mile canoe race that begins in San Marcos and ends at Seadrift on the Gulf Coast after clearing the Guadalupe River and crossing San Antonio Bay. Participants must transport all the gear they need with them, receiving only water, ice, and medical supplies along the way. They have 100 hours to complete the course, and possible complications and obstructions include dams, logjams, downed trees, alligators, water moccasins, mosquitos, fire ants, and sharks. There are 12 preestablished checkpoints, including the finish line. The fastest recorded team time is 29:46. The fastest recorded solo time is 36:03.

texaswatersafari.org

## INTREPID TEXAN

Beginning on September 1, 2021, *Texas Monthly* staffer Aaron Chamberlain cycled 3,014 miles in 58 days around the perimeter of Texas. That distance is more than Route 66 or the transcontinental route from NYC to Los Angeles. It could probably be traversed by car in one month, but buy Aaron a beer if you ever get to meet him. That quest epitomizes intrepid Textremity!

White Shaman Mural
Photo courtesy of E. R. Bills

# HISTORY AND CULTURE

44

# GET A GLIMPSE OF THE PLEISTOCENE AGE
## AT THE MAMMOTH NATIONAL MONUMENT

The Mammoth National Monument in Waco is the scene of an Ice Age mishap.

Approximately 67,000 years ago, a nursery herd of mammoths (6 adult females and 10 juveniles) died during a flash flood near the confluence of the Brazos and Bosque Rivers. They were buried in the mud and then, some 65,022 years later, two teenagers stumbled onto some of their bones while hunting for arrowheads. The rest, they say, is history. Or a fascinating glimpse into prehistory.

In July 2014, the resultant dig site became a national monument. It features a short, paved stroll and a climate-controlled viewing center, where the fossils can be observed in the arrangement they were discovered in.

Located just a few miles off Interstate 35, this remarkable find is a must-do in Central Texas.

6220 Steinbeck Bend Dr., Waco, TX 76708

nps.gov/waco/index.htm

### INTREPID TEXAN

A statue memorializing Waco native Doris "Dorie" Miller, the first African American to earn the Navy Cross, sits across town at the Bledsoe-Miller Park.

45

# TAKE IN
## THE ODESSA METEOR CRATER

In 1892, 12-year-old Julius D. Henderson rode his horse out in search of a lost calf. He located the wandering bovine grazing in an odd, oblong-shaped drop-off in the landscape and told his parents about it when he returned home.

In 1920, Elisha Virgil Graham discovered a peculiar, lava-like rock near the center of the sunken area. Graham gave the rock to his friend Samuel R. McKinney, the first mayor of Odessa. McKinney fancied the strange rock and used it as a paperweight in his office.

In 1922, A. C. Bibbins, a Baltimore geologist visiting the mayor's office on business, noticed the peculiar rock and examined it more closely. Bibbins declared that the paperweight was actually a meteorite, and McKinney permitted him to dislodge a shard and send it to George P. Merrill, the head curator of the Department of Geology at the US National Museum (now the Smithsonian National Museum of Natural History), for analysis. Merrill confirmed Bibbins's conclusion: the paperweight was a meteorite composed of extremely hard nickel-iron.

The Odessa Meteorite Crater became the second officially designated meteorite crater on Earth and was designated a National Natural Landmark on October 24, 1965.

Odessa Meteor Crater and Museum
3100 Meteor Crater Rd., Odessa, TX 79764
(432) 381-0946, odessameteorcrater.com

# DISCOVER
## THE ALIBATES FLINT QUARRIES NATIONAL MONUMENT

The Great Lakes are so large that one might think they appeared in North America before humans showed up, but that assumption is incorrect. The Great Lakes began forming around 14,000 years ago (at the end of the last glacial period), and before they developed into what they look like today, the people that plied the Texas Panhandle were already using flint in weapons and tools from what we now call the Alibates Flint Quarries. The durable, rainbow-hued flint from this site (just north of Amarillo) was widely sought after and traded across the region and throughout the Great Plains. High-quality arrowheads and spearheads were integral to human survival, especially for mammoth hunting.

The Alibates Flint Quarries site was the first national monument in Texas, and park personnel today offer fascinating short hikes and seasonal programs.

Cassjohnson Road, Fritch, TX 79036
(806) 857-6680, nps.gov/alfl/index.htm

### INTREPID TEXAN

Southeast of Perryton (an Ochiltree County town in the Panhandle), the remains of an ancient indigenous community referred to as "The Buried City" sits virtually unknown to most Texans. Tours of this fascinating site are only available through the Courson Archaeological Research Group.

47

# VISIT THE ALAMO

It's true the Alamo and the Texian Revolution have been controversially scrutinized of late, but politics around these parts is a contact sport, and every election season is an Alamo battle of sorts. Regardless of a visitor's disposition or personal leanings, the Alamo is an American icon harking back to a spirit of defiance that was prevalent across the Western frontier throughout the 19th century, and it has become the symbol for those who chose death over defeat midway through the war for Texas independence.

Originally known as the Mission San Antonio de Valero, the site was founded in 1718 by the Spanish to serve as a waystation between Mexico and East Texas. Though dwarfed by taller buildings around it, the 4.2-acre complex and the 50-foot cenotaph that lists the names of those who died in the Battle of the Alamo, receive more than 2.5 million visitors a year. Few leave the practical, spatial context for the legendary standoff uninspired.

300 Alamo Plaza, San Antonio, TX 78205
(210) 225-1391, thealamo.org

# WALK AROUND
## THE CADDO MOUNDS

The mythical expanse of Texas is difficult for many folks (including most Texans) to get their heads around, and most perceptions are based on the state since the Spanish laid claim to it in 1519. It's mind-boggling to think there could be more to Texas, but there is, and one of the best places to experience this revelation is at the Caddo Mounds State Historic Site. Located about 25 miles west of Nacogdoches, the 397-acre park is the only preserve of Caddo mounds in the state and features evidence of occupation for more than 12,000 years. A Southern Caddo Indian culture known as the Hasinai flourished in the area from around 800 A. D. to about 1300 A. D.

Unlike their hunter-gatherer precedents, the Hasinai arrived with highly developed horticultural methods and a fixed, complex culture. Their success and productivity fostered trade networks (stretching from the Gulf Coast to the Great Lakes), advanced social and political hierarchies, and large ceremonial centers. All that's left of the Hasinai at the site are three burial mounds and the remains of a "borrow pit," which was a human-made depression created during construction of the mounds.

Before six European, Mexican, Texan, and U.S. flags flew over Texas, the Caddo throve for almost 500 years, mastering agriculture, diplomacy, and early architecture in the region.

They created magnificent ceremonial blades and effigies and crafted some of the finest aboriginal ceramics on American soil, but their most famous contribution regards our nomenclature. The Hasinai called the first Spanish explorers they encountered "tayshas," meaning allies and friends. The Spanish later pronounced the word "tejas" and referred to the area as the Kingdom of Tejas.

1649 TX-21, Alto, TX 75925
(936) 858-3218
thc.texas.gov/historic-sites/caddo-mounds-state-historic-site

### INTREPID TEXAN

A great place to stay when you visit the Caddo Mounds is the beautiful 660-acre Mission Tejas State Park right down the road just seven miles west on State Hwy. 21.

tpwd.texas.gov/state-parks/mission-tejas

## 49

# EXAMINE
## THE ANCIENT INDIGENOUS AMERICAN PETROGLYPHS AT SEMINOLE CANYON

Humans began inhabiting the Seminole Canyon region 10,000 to 12,000 years ago and creating art on cave and bell shelter walls about 5,000 years later, continuing to add to their stone canvases until about 2,000 years ago. The renderings on the Fate Bell Shelter walls in particular are believed to be some of the oldest in North America.

Located about 45 miles west of Del Rio and just east of the impressive Pecos River High Bridge, the 2,173-acre Seminole Canyon State Park gets its name from the Black Seminole scouts who served in the region during the mid- to late 19th century. Today, this fascinating destination offers several campsites with basic amenities, guided tours of the Fate Bell Shelter, and other intriguing sights and hikes. Once there, you can also get information regarding the Amistad National Recreation Area boat tours, which allow folks to see the magnificent pictograph sites at the Panther and Parida caves.

U.S. Highway 90, Comstock, TX 78837
(432) 292-4464, tpwd.texas.gov/state-parks/seminole-canyon

50

# BEHOLD
## THE HEADLESS WHITE SHAMAN MURAL

Right down the road from Seminole Canyon on US-90 is the equally wondrous White Shaman Mural, which archaeologists now theorize depicts an indigenous Huichol or Nahua creation narrative linked to Uto-Aztec myths. Initially believed to be portraiture instructions for a prehistoric version of *The Electric Kool-Aid Acid Test* via peyote, the mural is thousands of years old and accessible only through tours conducted by the Witte Museum September through May every Saturday at 12:30 p.m. The colossal, prehistoric spreadsheet is 26 feet long and 13 feet tall in places, and features stirring, surreal anthropomorphic figures and the elongated headless human figure that gives the site its name. The rendering is unlike any other rock art on Earth and, like the Fate Bell Shelter, should not be missed.

wittemuseum.org/white-shaman-preserve

# WONDER
## AT THE JOHNSON SPACE CENTER

Located 25 miles southeast of Houston on Interstate 45, the 1,600-acre Johnson Space Center is the official headquarters and training base for American astronauts, the site of Mission Control for the International Space Station, and home of the Orion Program, which is currently sorting out the logistics of deep space flight for future missions to Mars and other space-related endeavors. For almost four decades, every NASA astronaut and any space explorer from partner nations who has spent time at the International Space Station or been part of a space shuttle team has received his or her training at the Johnson Space Center. The importance of this facility can't be overstated, and 90-minute tram tours, which include an Astronaut Training Facility Tour and a Mission Control Center Tour, are offered seven days a week.

nasa.gov/centers/johnson/home/index.html

NASA Space Suits at Johnson Space Center
Carol M. Highsmith America/Library of Congress

Abandoned, old US-180 in the Guadalupe Mountains
Photo courtesy of E. R. Bills

Giant, "trunkless legs of stone" that comprise the "Ozymandias on the Plains" near Amarillo
Photo courtesy of Wednesday Tijerina

Milky Way above Terlinga Ruins
Photo courtesy of Nick Quinn Photograhy

Beachcombing Cowboy on Galveston Beach
Photo courtesy of E. R. Bills

Bear Crossing at Big Bend
Photo courtesy of E. R. Bills

Texas State Aquarium
Photo courtesy of Texas State Aquarium

San Antonio River Walk
Photo courtesy of Mark Bonica

Buddy Holly Statue
Photo courtesy of E. R. Bills

Corpus Christi Causeway Cabin
Photo courtesy of E. R. Bills

Stevie Ray Vaughan
Photo courtesy of Alamy

## INTREPID TEXAN

"While I was sleeping, I had a beautiful dream that all the people of the world got together on the same wavelength and began helping each other." —Stevie Ray Vaughan (October 3, 1954–August 27, 1990)

Bull riding
Photo courtesy of Cowtown Coliseum

# EXPERIENCE
## THE FORT WORTH STOCKYARDS

The Stockyards National Historic District in Fort Worth is one of the most popular tourist destinations in Texas. Folks come from all over the world to get a glimpse of the Old West, and the Stockyards capably oblige. Local cowboys drive Texas Longhorn cattle through the redbrick streets every day at 11:30 a.m. and 4:00 p.m. The world's largest honky-tonk, Billy Bob's Texas, is open every night, and the Stockyards Championship Rodeo is staged every weekend (at 8:00 p.m. on Friday and Saturday). The intervals can be filled with visits to any number of historic buildings, bars, restaurants, shops, and other attractions, including the Texas Cowboy Hall of Fame, the Stockyards Museum, the White Elephant Saloon, and M. L. Leddy's, which has been crafting handmade boots, saddles, belts, and buckles since 1922.

### INTREPID TEXAN

The National Cowgirl Museum and Hall of Fame is also located in Fort Worth, about 10 minutes away from the Stockyards (at 720 Gendy St.).
cowgirl.net

Tornado over Capitol
Photo courtesy of Austin History Center,
Austin Public Library

# SEE
## THE TEXAS STATE CAPITOL

One hundred years ago, a tornado formed over the Texas State Capitol but did little damage. These days, cataclysms and calamities seem to emanate the edifice, but it's still standing. Completed in 1888, the structure was the seventh-largest building in the world and stood seven feet taller than its national counterpart in Washington, D.C. Transporting the pink granite (from Marble Falls) necessary to construct the exterior alone required 15,000 railroad cars, and the interior woodwork was crafted from several linear miles of the highest quality mahogany, walnut, ash, cedar, pine, and oak in the region. The terrazo-floored Capitol rotunda displays paintings and sculptures of noteworthy Lone Star leaders, and a $75 million underground extension was completed in 1993. Tours of the Capitol are available every day, and events such as the annual Texas Book Festival are held on the surrounding grounds.

1100 Congress Ave., Austin, TX 78701
tspb.texas.gov/prop/tc/tc/capitol.html

### INTREPID TEXAN

Just east of the Capitol, the Texas State Library and Archives Commission is an incredible resource for general cultural and historical research.
tsl.texas.gov

# INSPECT
## THE SIXTH FLOOR MUSEUM

On November 22, 1963, Texas became the site of one of the darkest acts in American history. John F. Kennedy, the 35th president of the United States, was assassinated in broad daylight as he rode in a presidential motorcade through Dallas. The crime has never been satisfactorily investigated, explained, or put to rest, and this brazen act traumatized the nation in ways we still don't fully understand. The Kennedy assassination essentially eclipses almost everything else that Dallas, the ninth-largest city in the United States, has to offer. Half a million folks visit the Sixth Floor Museum and the grassy knoll every year, trying to make sense of it. The museum offers viewings of the Zapruder film, oral histories, a Jack Ruby collection, and special exhibits.

411 Elm St., Dallas, TX 75202
(214) 747-6660, jfk.org

### INTREPID TEXAN

Take some time to wander around Dealey Plaza and the grassy knoll on foot. The gravity of the site and the implications of the act still reverberate.

# LEARN MORE
## ABOUT THE BUFFALO SOLDIERS AT FORT DAVIS

The indigenous peoples of Texas were a fierce lot, so it probably wouldn't be fair to say that they feared any enemy, but they had a healthy respect for a new warrior that appeared in Fort Davis in 1867.

Comprising one half of the ninth U.S. Cavalry at Fort Davis, their Native American foes called them "Buffalo Soldiers" because of their coarse, curly hair and ferocity in battle. These African American troops manned the last fights against the Apache in Texas and were then transferred to the Arizona Territory, where they helped subdue Geronimo.

The 523-acre Fort Davis National Historic Site is a good place to familiarize oneself with how the Buffalo Soldiers lived and fought. It is also one of the best preserved examples of a frontier military outpost in the Southwest.

101 Lt. Flipper Dr. #1379, Fort Davis, TX 79734
(432) 426-3224, nps.gov/foda/index.htm

### INTREPID TEXAN

The Davis Mountains State Park right up State Hwy. 118 is home to the outstanding adobe-style Indian Lodge hotel and eight dozen great mile-high camping spots. It is also close to the McDonald Observatory and the town of Fort Davis.

56

# VISIT
## THE SAN JACINTO BATTLEGROUND STATE HISTORIC SITE

At first mention, it could be argued that this stop is a formality attraction. Yes, Sam Houston and the Texian fighters defeated Santa Anna here on April 21, 1836, but the battlefield itself is just a green space without compelling particulars, and the most notable aspect of the 567-foot-tall San Jacinto Monument, which stands alongside the Houston Ship Channel, is that it's almost 13 feet taller than the Washington Monument.

The real star of the complex is the State Historic Site's museum ship, the USS *Texas*. Also referred to as "Battleship Texas," the USS *Texas* was the first American battleship to be declared a National Historic Landmark, the first American battleship to be converted into a museum ship, the only surviving World War I–era dreadnought battleship, and one of the only remaining ships that served in both World Wars. Seeing the USS *Texas* from the 489-foot-tall observation floor of the San Jacinto Monument (reached by elevator) is interesting, but boarding the vessel itself and exploring the main and lower decks is mind-blowing. The historical context, the practical details, the cramped bunks, the gun stations—it's imagination-provoking, riveting stuff.

3523 Independence Pkwy., La Porte, TX 77571
(281) 479-2431, tpwd.texas.gov/state-parks/san-jacinto-battleground

# MARVEL
## AT THE IMMACULATE CONCEPTION CATHEDRAL

Dedicated in July 1856, the Gothic revival–style Immaculate Conception Cathedral in Brownsville is still composed of 250,000 of the original handmade bricks and retains 29 original stained-glass windows majestically depicting dramatic scenes from the Bible (ranging from the namesake Immaculate Conception to Jesus being taken down from the cross). It also still has the original wooden pews, which comfortably seat almost 400.

Its magnificent chandeliers, which hang from the vaulted, blue nave ceilings, were shipped over from France in 1865, and it is home to an antique pipe organ that arrived in 1935.

Listed in the National Register of Historic Places in 1980, the Immaculate Conception Cathedral is a stunning monument to the Catholic faith and the miracle the cathedral is named for.

1218 E. Jefferson St., Brownsville, TX 78520
(956) 546-3178, immaculateconceptioncathedral.org

### INTREPID TEXAN

The backstory behind the Cathedral's architect, Father Pierre Yves Kéralum, is amazing. He completed the structure after the original supervisor, Father Superior Jean Verdet, disappeared at sea. Then, decades later, Kéralum disappeared himself.

# TRACE THE FOOTSTEPS OF DOC HOLLIDAY AND WYATT EARP AT FORT GRIFFIN

Fans of the Old West could hardly do better than a stop at the Fort Griffin State Historic Site in Shackelford County. Fort Griffin sat on a hill just north of present-day Albany, and the settlement that sprang up at the base of the hill became known as the "Babylon of the West." Legendary lawman Wyatt Earp met Doc Holliday there, and they became fast friends. The community bustled with cowboys, gunfighters, gamblers, buffalo hunters, and "painted ladies," including John Wesley Hardin, John Selman, Lottie Deno, and Big Nose Kate. From 1874 to 1878, Fort Griffin was the largest city between Dallas and El Paso and an important station on the Great Western Trail.

Today, there isn't much left, but what is there is picturesque and easy to peruse. The park office even offers complimentary golf carts to tour the hill. History buffs can easily spend a whole day here, examining the sites of the Bush Knob Massacre, the Butterfield Stage Clear Fork Station, Daws Crossing, and the intersection of the aforementioned Great Western Trail and the Goodnight-Loving Trail. The State Historic Site is also the home of the Official State of Texas Longhorn Herd.

1701 N. U.S. Hwy. 283, Albany, TX 76430
(325) 762-3592, thc.texas.gov/historic-sites/fort-griffin-state-historic-site

Wyatt Earp, 1869
Photo courtesy of Wikimedia Commons

# SEE JEFFERSON

This Marion County treasure near the eastern edge of Texas is tough to beat for a weekend getaway. The weekly Ghost Walk, mostly conducted in the well-preserved downtown, is wildly entertaining (even for skeptics). Then, there's a haunted hotel (Excelsior House), which you can test your mettle by staying in, and the Grove, which is hands-down (or flailing at your side as you flee) the most haunted place in Texas.

The town is also home to the nostalgic Jefferson General Store, the fascinating Jefferson Historic Museum, the historic House of the Seasons, a *Gone With the Wind* museum, and one of the last remaining Carnegie Libraries (that's still in operation) in Texas.

Jefferson also offers access to swamp tours, bayou tours, and great fishing at Caddo Lake or Lake O' the Pines. Is your overnight bag ready yet?

## INTREPID TEXAN

Wiley College, home of the "Great Debaters," is only 17 miles south on US Hwy. 59 in the city of Marshall.

# EXPLORE GUSHERS
## AT THE EAST TEXAS OIL MUSEUM

Way before HBO's *Westworld*, there was "Eastworld" at the East Texas Oil Museum. Located on the campus of Kilgore College, the facility features a life-size indoor replica of a 1930s boomtown, complete with primitive human animatrons in vintage automobiles and trucks and a horse-drawn carriage, all stuck in the mud. The museum also includes life-size models of a general store, a machine shop, a barber shop, post office, drugstore, gas station, cinema, and an "Elevator Ride to the Center of the Earth." The animated residents haunt the place, especially the barber.

To date, the East Texas Oil Field has produced 6 billion barrels of oil, and, at the height of the oil boom, more than 1,100 producing wooden oil derricks sat inside the Kilgore city limits. Oil production has obviously slowed down, but the Kilgore boomtown lives on.

1301 S. Henderson Blvd., Kilgore, TX 75662
903) 983-8295, easttexasoilmuseum.kilgore.edu

# JAM WITH JANIS
## AT THE MUSEUM OF THE GULF COAST

The Museum of the Gulf Coast is devoted to Port Arthur's most famous native, 1960s rock icon Janis Joplin. A misfit in her hometown and the subject of no small amount of scorn and ridicule at the University of Texas, Joplin moved to California and became a superstar in the music world, belting out psychedelic blues and gut-wrenching soul as powerfully as few artists before or since. Her exhibit includes photos, memorabilia, and a full-size replica of the Queen of Rock and Roll's 1965 Porsche.

The museum is also home to a music hall of fame that recognizes local-born talents such as Joplin, Clarence "Gatemouth" Brown, Edgar Winter, and George Jones, and a sports hall of fame that celebrates legends such as Babe Didrikson Zaharias and former Dallas Cowboys head coach Jimmy Johnson. The facility also includes works from influential local-born artist Robert Rauschenberg.

700 Procter St., Port Arthur, TX 77640
(409) 982-7000, museumofthegulfcoast.org

### INTREPID TEXAN

Sea Rim State Park is just 24 miles away down State Hwy. 87. It's one of the few places you can see alligators up close and hang out on a beach at the same location.

# LEARN THE TRUTH
## ABOUT THE TRUER DER UNION MONUMENT

In 1862, the Confederate States of America declared martial law in Central Texas, due to significant resistance to the Civil War. Jacob Kuechler, a surveyor of German descent and conscientious objector to the war, agreed to serve as a guide for 61 other conscientious objectors (mostly German) attempting to escape the reach of Confederate conscription by fleeing to Mexico. Confederate irregulars caught them at the Nueces River and killed 34, taking the rest prisoner.

On August 10, 1866, a 20-foot-tall obelisk, funded by donations from local residents and families of the victims, was dedicated in Comfort, Texas. The main structure weighs 35,700 pounds and includes four tablets listing the victims' names. A 36-star American flag—representing the number of states in the Union at the time of the dedication—flies over the site.

Comfort, TX 78013 (High Street, between Third and Fourth)

### INTREPID TEXAN

A large percentage of the immigrants who settled the Comfort area were known as *Freidenkers* or "freethinkers." The Comfort freethinkers were irreligious and advocated reason and democracy over religious and political authoritarianism. The community didn't have a church for the first 40 years of its existence.

# FENCE YOURSELF IN
## AT THE DEVIL'S ROPE MUSEUM

When barbed wire (the Devil's Rope) was first introduced by big ranchers in Texas in 1875, Texans weren't having it. Cattle drives required access to public land and public water sources, and rank-and-file Texans despised fencing off the frontier. They began sneaking out at night and cutting down miles of barbed wire fencing as fast at the big ranches put it up. It led to what became known as the Fence-Cutter's War, where the big ranches hired private security and poached Texas Rangers from the state to police the fence lines of their property. In the end, the frontier, the cattle drivers and, arguably, true Texans, lost—hence, the devilish moniker.

The Devil's Rope Museum showcases every variety of barbed wire, including "entanglement" wires from modern American wars.

100 Kingsley St., McLean, TX 79057
(806) 779-2225, barbwiremuseum.com

### INTREPID TEXAN

The abandoned Old Dixie Motel and Restaurant sits a few minutes east on 1st Street. Its fortunes faded when Interstate 40 replaced historic Route 66.

# REMEMBER THE AUTHOR
## OF THE GREAT SOCIETY

The Vietnam War ruined the broader legacy of the 36th president of the United States, Lyndon Baines Johnson. This is unfortunate because his legislative accomplishments are unparalleled in modern history.

During LBJ's 63-month term in office, he signed four Civil Rights acts, four Environmental Protections acts, three Wilderness Protection acts, three Transportation acts, two Higher Education acts, two Economic Opportunity acts, two food protection acts, one Endangered Species Act, one Historic Preservation act, a National Foundation on the Arts and Humanities Act (which created the National Endowment for the Arts and the National Endowment for the Humanities), a Public Broadcasting Act (which led to the creation of National Public Radio), a Bilingual Education act, a Truth-in-Lending act, the first Cigarette Labeling and Advertising Act (mandating health warnings), and a Social Security act that authorized Medicare. Love him or hate him or both, LBJ's aggressive flurry of domestic programs was enacted to foster a "Great Society" for all, and he remains the boldest, most progressive political leader America has ever produced. The 1,571-acre Lyndon B. Johnson National Historical Park in Stonewall is a great place to consider his legacy.

199 Park Road 52, Stonewall, TX 78671
tpwd.texas.gov/state-parks/lyndon-b-johnson

65

# PAY YOUR RESPECTS
## AT MONUMENT HILL

Lots of folks today—including too many Texans—forget that our troubles with Santa Anna didn't end after his defeat at the hands of Sam Houston on April 21, 1836, or even after he signed the Treaty of Velasco, which recognized Texas independence a few weeks later. In 1842, Santa Anna (who had regained the Mexican presidency a year earlier) began encouraging his military to begin raids into Texas to destabilize the young nation and discourage foreign investment. San Antonio was seized by Mexican troops twice in 1842, and during the second go-round, Texans responded with force. Though the confrontations led to Mexican withdrawal, three dozen Texans perished at Dawson's Creek, and several more died during the ill-fated Mier Expedition. In 1848, their remains were collected and interred in a common tomb in a sandstone vault at what is now known as the Monument Hill State Historic Site, which shares its seven-acre location with the Kreische Brewery State Historic Site.

As part of the Texas Centennial celebrations in 1936, a 48-foot-tall monument adorned with an Art Deco mural was placed to mark the grave. Besides being a great place to learn the whole story and pay your respects, Monument Hill also offers nice hikes and impressive views of the Colorado River.

414 TX-92 Spur, La Grange, TX 78945
tpwd.texas.gov/state-parks/monument-hill-kreische-brewery

66

# RETURN TO TEXAS
## AT THE GREENWOOD CEMETERY

Texas literary giant Larry McMurtry borrowed a substantial portion of the plotline for *Lonesome Dove* from the life of Oliver Loving, a longtime partner of Charles Goodnight. Loving established the Goodnight-Loving Trail with Charles, and they participated in several cattle ventures together. On their last drive, Loving and a scout went ahead of the herd to negotiate a contract but were attacked by Native Americans. Loving was injured but made it to Fort Sumner, where he died of gangrene.

Goodnight had promised Loving that his remains would be returned to Texas if he died outside the state and, after temporary interment at Fort Sumner (while Goodnight got the herd to Colorado), Loving's body was exhumed and returned to Texas, where it was reburied at Greenwood Cemetery in Weatherford.

Black cowboy Bose Ikard, the man *Lonesome Dove*'s "Joshua Deets" is based on (played by Danny Glover), is also buried at Greenwood Cemetery.

Located behind the Parker County Jail in Weatherford, just off Fort Worth Highway.

67

# CHANGE HISTORY
## AT AVENGER FIELD

The Stinson sisters in San Antonio trained male pilots to fly in World War I but were prohibited from joining the fray. Beginning in November 1942, more than 1,000 women were trained to fly in the early stages of World War II and transferred to Avenger Field. As part of the Women's Auxiliary Ferrying Squadron and Women's Flying Training Detachment (WASP), female pilots flew every aircraft in the Army's arsenal, towing gunnery targets, transporting equipment, ferrying, and flight-testing repaired aircraft to make sure they were airworthy for the WASP's male counterparts. For more than two years, the WASP served at more than 120 bases around the country and suffered only 37 casualties in the line of duty.

In June 1944, Army Air Forces Commanding General Henry Harley "Hap" Arnold sought to officially designate the WASP as members of the United States Military, but the US Congress declined his request. After a lengthy battle with their own government, the WASP were granted military status in 1977, thanks to a bill signed by President Jimmy Carter.

The National WASP WWII Museum in Sweetwater features some of the actual aircraft the WASP flew, photographs, memorabilia, and oral histories. It is the best place in the country to familiarize yourself with WASP history.

210 Avenger Field Rd., Sweetwater, TX 79556
(325) 235-0099, waspmuseum.org

# INSPECT
## THE TEXAS RANGER HALL OF FAME AND MUSEUM

There's not a more iconic American law enforcement institution than the legendary Texas Rangers. Most of us were first introduced to them in the television series *The Lone Ranger*, which ran from 1949 to 1957, and children were still watching the serial well into the 1970s. Since 1910, almost 400 American movies have featured a Texas Ranger as a main character, and recent memory immediately conjures up such critically acclaimed classics as *No Country for Old Men* (2007), the remake of *True Grit* (2010), and *Hell or High Water* (2016).

Rangers retain statewide jurisdiction and have served as a policing arm and a paramilitary force in service of the Republic of Texas and the State of Texas. They have waged war, patrolled the border, provided security for the governor, broke up race riots, and ended the crime sprees of countless outlaws (including Sam Bass and Bonnie and Clyde). Historically speaking, they have always been a formidable force, usually for the good—but not always.

The Texas Ranger Hall of Fame and Museum is a great place to learn about their role and legacy in Lone Star history.

100 Texas Ranger Trail, Waco, TX 76706
(254) 750-8631, texasranger.org

Cooper's Old Time Pit Barbecue
Photo courtesy of E. R. Bills

# FOOD AND DRINK

# EXPLORE
## YOUR TEX-MEX ROOTS

The late 18th and early 19th century French gastronic philosopher Jean Anthelme Brillat-Savarin once claimed that if you told him what you ate, he could tell you what you are. If Brillat-Savarin were diagnosing the diets of most Texans today, he might tell us we're Mexican . . . or at least half-Mexican.

Yes, Mexicans prefer white cheese and corn tortillas, and Texans splurge on yellow cheese and choose flour tortillas and sometimes black beans, but there's more crossover than separation . . . and that's the way it should be. Tex-Mex is the perfect culinary embodiment of who Texans really are, embracing our minor differences and celebrating our major similarities. The kitchen truth of the matter sets us all free, and we celebrate it daily at breakfast, lunch, and dinner.

**L & J Café (El Paso)**
Located on the east side of El Paso, this go-to eatery is next to the old graveyard and just off Interstate I-10.

3622 E. Missouri Ave., El Paso, TX 79903
(915) 566-8418, landjcafe.com

**Herbert's Taco Hut (San Marcos)**
Located right off Interstate 35, a San Marcos and Texas State University Rugby favorite for 30 years.

419 Riverside Dr., San Marcos, TX 78666
(512) 392-2993, herbertstacohutsanmarcos.com

**Angie's (Austin)**
Old school Tex-Mex in a fun part of town.

1307 E 7th St., Austin, TX 78702
512-476-5413

**El Milagrito Café (San Antonio)**
Authentic neighborhood Tex-Mex with huevos rancheros morir por.

521 E. Woodlawn Ave., San Antonio, TX 78212
(210) 737-8646

**Benito's Restaurant (Fort Worth)**
Best pico around for decades, reasonable prices, and sometimes live mariachi on Saturday nights.

1450 W. Magnolia Ave., Fort Worth, TX 76104
(817) 332-8633, benitosmexican.com

**YaYa's Place (Hillsboro)**
Perfect for a Central Texas taco fix!

116 North Waco Street, Hillsboro, TX 76645
(254) 582-3999

# EXPERIENCE
## BBQ NIRVANA

"Barbecue may not be the road to world peace, but it's a start." Thus spake the late, great Anthony Bourdain, the world's foremost ambassador for culinary exploration.

Here in Texas, the roads to BBQ may be paved, pea gravel, or red dirt, but they always arrive at an amicable space for a mealtime kumbaya. The Dalai Lama of Texas BBQ is beef brisket, smoked until fall-apart tender and usually seasoned enough by wet or dry rubs and its own natural fats that sauce is optional. In fact, beef brisket is even moonlighting in tacos and nachos these days, subtly threatening a separation of church and state.

Beef ribs also offer enlightenment, and most pit masters will begrudgingly offer a pork, chicken, or sausage option and the occasional slab of smoked bologna. Potato salad, pinto beans, and a slice or two of white bread are the customary sides.

**Goldee's Barbecue (Kennedale)**
The new number one!

4645 Dick Price Rd., Fort Worth, TX 76140
(817) 480-4131, goldeesbbq.com

**Burnt Bean Co. (Seguin)**
Open Thursday through Sunday until they sell out.

108 S. Austin St., Seguin, TX 78155
burntbeanco.com

**Cattleack BBQ**
So good they're only open two days a week.

13628 Gamma Rd., Farmers Branch, TX 75244

(972) 805-0999, cattleackbbq.com

**Cooper's Old Time Pit Bar-B-Que (Llano)**
Worth the detour to Llano, but the only thing green on the menu is jalapeños.

604 W. Young St., Llano, TX 78643
(325) 247-5713, coopersbbq.com

**Franklin Barbecue (Austin)**

An Austin favorite, but open for lunch only; better get there four hours early.

900 E. 11th St., Austin, TX 78702
(512) 653-1187, franklinbbq.com

**BBQ on the Brazos (Cresson)**

Kicks tastebuds in Cresson!

9001 E US Hwy. 377, Cresson, TX 76035
(817) 396-0379, bbqonthebrazoscressontx.com

71

# EAT SOME CHICKEN FRIED STEAK (IT'S THE LAW)

In his 1968 meditation on the state of the state—*In a Narrow Grave: Essays on Texas*—Larry McMurtry put it plainly: "Only a rank degenerate would drive 1,500 miles across Texas without eating a chicken fried steak."

He was right, of course, and one sunny day in May 43 years later, the Texas State Legislature resolved that it be so in HR 1419. To wit (and paraphrased): "WHEREAS, Texans are renowned for their love of chicken fried steak, that exceptional dish that elevates the hearty flavor of beef to new heights by coating it in batter and breading and frying it until the ingredients are melded in a blissful union" and "WHEREAS, generations of Lone Star State residents have partaken of this beloved entrée" and "WHEREAS, this signature dish occupies a special place in the culinary culture of the Lone Star State, and Texas Chicken Fried Steak Day provides a welcome opportunity to pay homage to that shared legacy; now, therefore, be it RESOLVED, that the House of Representatives of the 82nd Texas Legislature hereby recognize October 26, 2011, as Texas Chicken Fried Steak Day and extend sincere best wishes to all who are taking part in this unique occasion."

The official holiday has passed, but you can still partake of the "beloved entrée" practically everywhere on Texas soil.

**Mary's Café**

Seventy miles west of Fort Worth and 70 miles east of Abilene, Mary's is the longtime reigning champ of quintessential chicken fried steak.

119 Grant Ave., Strawn, TX 76475
(254) 672-5741

**Gristmill River Restaurant & Bar**

A rising challenger located in an 1878 cotton gin with a shady patio and views of the Guadalupe River.

1287 Gruene Rd., New Braunfels, TX 78130
(830) 625-0684, gristmillrestaurant.com

**Miller's Seawall Grill**

Location, location, location. Chicken fried steak right across the street from the beach.

1824 Seawall Blvd., Galveston, TX 77550
(409) 763-8777, millersseawallgrillgalveston.com

**Goodson's Cafe**

Making "World Famous" chicken fried steak since it opened its doors in the mid-1950s.

27931 Tomball Parkway, Tomball, TX 77377
(281) 351-1749, goodsonscafe.com

**Jake and Dorothy's Cafe (Stephenville)**

Generous plates in a down-to-earth setting.

406 E. Washington St., Stephenville, TX 76401
(254) 965-5211

**Lucile's (Fort Worth)**

Right off redbrick Camp Bowie and tough to beat.

4700 Camp Bowie Blvd., Fort Worth, TX 76107
(817) 738-4761, luciles.org

# GET GIDDY
## AT GILHOOLEY'S

Gilhooley's Restaurant and Oyster Bar atmosphere may be curmudgeonly, but its food offerings are quite amicable. For years, it refused to accept credit cards and prohibited children; credit cards are now okay, but children are still out of luck. But that's what an eatery can do if the Travel Channel refers to it as the "ultimate seafood dive."

The no-frills restaurant's specialty is Oysters Gilhooley, a dozen pit-smoked oysters generously drenched in garlic butter and topped with Parmesan cheese, but the seafood joint also offers a fried oyster dinner, a fried oyster po'boy, barbecued oysters, a seasonal oyster stew, raw oysters, fried shrimp, barbecued crab, seafood cakes, and a full, horseshoe-shaped bar—which is important because even grouchy regulars begrudgingly admit that everything on the menu goes well with a longneck beer and a side of hush puppies.

222 9th St., San Leon, TX 77539
(281) 339-3813, gilhooleystx.com

73

# GET YOUR DUE
## AT DREW'S

A hole in the wall in West Fort Worth for years, Drew's Place has never tried real hard to be fancy, but don't let the function-over-form atmosphere fool you. Drew's calling card is mouthwatering soul food, comfort cuisine, and stick-to-your-ribs grub, par excellence—because you've earned it.

Most eateries would be thrilled to enjoy universal appreciation for just one of their signature dishes, but Drew's bowls customers over with two. Drew's serves (1) the Best Fried Chicken in Texas and (2) the Best Smothered Pork Chops in Texas. The restaurant also serves up a mean meat loaf, oxtail, collard greens, candied yams, boiled cabbage, and an excellent glass of sweet tea. And did I mention the desserts?

5701 Curzon, Fort Worth, TX 76107
(817) 242-4454, drewssoulfoodfw.com

74

# CHECK OUT
## THE CZECH STOP

At one time, the only attention the small town of West received was for sitting near the site of the Crash at Crush, an 1896 Katy Railroad publicity stunt that involved the intentional collision of two railroad engines. These days, the collision this community is most known for is culinary.

Not too long ago, when any normal, red-blooded Texan walked into a doughnut shop, all he or she saw on the menu was doughnuts (and maybe cinnamon rolls).

Talk about a culture shift.

Today, you can't find a doughnut shop that doesn't offer kolaches, and such eateries as the Czech Stop and Little Czech Bakery can take a lot of the credit. The deli/bakery thrills several hundred kolache-crazy customers a day, and they're open 24 hours a day, seven days a week.

105 N. College St., West, TX 76691
(254) 826-4161, czechstop.net

75

# EAT
## AT THE OLD ORANGE CAFÉ

Located in the southwest center of downtown Orange (and just a few blocks from a crazy bend in the Sabine River), the Old Orange Café sits in the community's old dairy building, which closed down in 1948. Open for lunch every day except Saturday, it offers a mean country fried steak, a tasty Cajun-smothered catfish, and a good assortment of burgers and sandwiches. The desserts are scrumptious, the service is down-home, and a marker-highlighted line around the interior walls indicates where the waters peaked during the last flood swell.

The Old Orange Café is worth a visit even if the Sabine is up. Just bring a life preserver.

914 W. Division, Orange, Texas 77630
(409) 883-2233, oldorangecafe.com

# HUMBLE YOURSELF
## AT HERD'S

It used to be the only way you got a burger at Herd's Burgers in Jacksboro was how they served it. The hamburger meat was scooped, slung, and cooked to juicy perfection with a cement trowel, but the choice of sliced vegetables (usually lettuce, tomato, onion, and pickle) and condiments included on the burger was the cook's decision. The only side was a plain bag of potato chips. It was a Herd's Burger or no burger.

These days customers have some say as to what gets added to their juicy burgers, and they can select fries with their order instead of a bag of chips, but there's something really Texan about not being picky or finicky, and feeling nostalgic about the old Herd's (which opened in 1916) is okay. Of course, you can still leave the call to the cook. Either way, Herd's Burgers is a Texas institution regardless of its menu evolution.

400 North Main St., Jacksboro, TX 76458

### INTREPID TEXAN

After your burger, sneak by the Fort Richardson State Park and Historic Site.
tpwd.texas.gov/state-parks/fort-richardson

77

# GRAB A CHAIR
## AT THE TEXAS CHILI PARLOR

Decisions, decisions, decisions. Habanero beef chili, black bean and sausage chili, white pork chili, five-bean veggie chili, or a three-bowl chili taster. Or a chili potato. Or Frito pie.

In a perfect world, every state would have its own chili parlor, and some do. In this imperfect world, at least we have our own, and it's been cooking up chili since 1976. This culinary landmark doesn't serve up deer chili, elk chili, or technically even traditional Texas chili—just mouthwatering variations on the theme—which is why the eatery is referred to as a parlor rather than a café or diner. Unlike most parlors, however, this one offers a well-stocked bar and stays open until 2:00 a.m.

Grab a stool and dig in. The Austin ambiance is on the house.

1409 Lavaca St., Austin, TX 78701
(512) 472-2828

Roy Orbison catching a plane in 1965
Photo courtesy of Jack de Nijs / Anefo, Wikipedia Commons

# ROAD TRIPS

78

# SPANISH FORT

When you see the town of Spanish Fort on a Texas map, it jumps out at you. It's tucked into a long bend of the Red River, just north of Nocona. You know—or at least think you know—that the Spanish didn't have any forts that far north in Texas. You wonder if the structure is still intact. You wonder why you've never heard of it before.

Your initial curiosity is rewarded by fascinating revelations.

First, the fort, which included wooden stockades, entrenchments, and a moat (yes, a moat—in Texas) is long gone. An Art Deco historical marker stands on the original location. Second, "Spanish" fort is wholly inaccurate. The fortification was actually a French structure built at the location of a preexisting Taovaya Indian village around 1719. The Taovaya had just moved into the region when the French were beginning to venture farther west along the Red River, and the two peoples quickly became successful trading partners. Third, when the only major defense of the fort was mounted in 1759, the attacking forces were actually Spanish, and the fort defenders were Taovaya, Wichita, and Comanche Indians, joined and at least rudimentarily trained by a small French contingent. When an early Anglo settler visited the ruins 100 years later, he simply assumed they were

Spanish, hence the town name "Spanish Fort." Finally, the Native American rout of the Spanish at the French Taovaya fortress marked Spain's earliest defeat in Texas and probably kept them from expanding farther north.

The drive up from Nocona features hundreds of active oil industry pump jacks, and the site of Spanish Fort is intriguing but desolate—basically a ghost town itself.

Take FM 103 north out of Nocona

### INTREPID TEXAN

Many foreign and out-of-state (i.e., also foreign) visitors love taking pictures in front of and on the abovementioned oil industry pump jacks. Photography is fine, but do not climb or stand on the equipment. It engages and operates intermittently and sends no small number of tourists to the hospital or the grave.

79

# STATUE OF OLD YELLER

In classic Texas movies, such as *The Searchers*, the Lone Star state got credit for many panoramic vistas that weren't actually located here, but we give as good as we get.

Most people forget or never realized that *Old Yeller* was a Texas story. Its author, Fred Gipson, was born near Mason on February 7, 1908. As a young man, Gipson worked on several local farms and ranches until he enrolled at the University of Texas in 1933. Gipson's first book, *The Fabulous Empire: Colonel Zack Miller's Story*, appeared in 1946, and his second book, *Hound-Dog Man*, came out in 1947. *Hound-Dog Man* was named to the popular Doubleday Book-of-the-Month Club and sold more than 250,000 copies in its first year. *Old Yeller* was published in 1956 and made into a successful Walt Disney film a year later. The motion picture portrayal of Old Yeller's passing is considered one of the saddest moments in cinematic history.

Mason County M. Beven Eckert Memorial Library
410 Post Hill St., Mason, TX 76856
mason.ploud.net

# REGENCY SUSPENSION BRIDGE

When you step onto the one-lane Regency Suspension Bridge, located at the intersection of Mills County Road 433 and San Saba County Road 137, it doesn't take long to figure out why they call the 340-foot-long structure the "swinging bridge." The wood-planked span moves under your weight, and then you watch, mouth agape, as cars and trucks drive across it.

The first bridge over the Colorado River at this spot was constructed in 1903, later collapsing under the weight of a crossing cattle herd. The second bridge was washed away by flooding in 1936. The structure we see today was a public works project completed in 1939, and it's one of the neatest little attractions in Texas.

Bypassed by modern, paved thoroughfares, reaching the Regency requires traversing miles of dirt road. When you finally get there, you should immediately cross the bridge in your sub-5,000 pound vehicle. Because once you feel how much it moves under your individual weight, you may be disinclined to drive over it. Either way, once atop the bridge, you can survey a long stretch of the Colorado River from either side.

# STAY
## IN A SMALL TOWN

Several years back, I stopped in the quiet, Gulf Coast town of Palacios and learned something I never knew.

In 1973, folks were reporting UFOs in the skies all across America. People were fascinated, freaking out, or fearful. But W. C. "Bill" Jackson, the mayor of Palacios, was philosophical. On October 19, he offered the aliens (who were presumably operating these mysterious crafts) sanctuary. "It just occurred to me that no one has ever made those little fellas welcome," Mayor Jackson said. "So we—the town council—issued a proclamation to make it official. It is my belief that every traveler needs a home away from home."

Local reaction was positive, and Jackson called on President Richard Nixon to declare Palacios the Interplanetary Capital of the Universe. Then, on Wednesday, October 24, 1973, the small Palacios Airport held the First Annual UFO Fly-In Day!

There are hundreds of small towns in Texas. If you already live in a small town in Texas, visit another one. If you have already visited one, visit a second. Stay in the hotels or motels. Eat at the mom-and-pop restaurants, buy something from a small-town shop, support a local craftsperson. Meet the people, chat up them up, and listen to their stories. They're members of a vanishing breed. If you don't go, you'll never know.

## SOME TOWNS TO VISIT

**Sanderson (Pop. 837)**

As Texas travel writer Pam Leblanc puts it, this "underrated, adventurous" census-designated county seat "on the edge of the Big Bend region has a trendy motel, pistol-packing waitresses, and starry nights aplenty."

**Edom (Pop. 335)**

Twenty miles east of Tyler, Edom is an artsy town with recharging nature retreats and good food options.

**Canadian (Pop. 2,786)**

Home of the magnificent Palace Theater, this High Plains oasis is near the Gene Howe Wildlife Management Area and the Black Kettle National Grasslands.

**Bandera (Pop. 671)**

This cowboy town boasts a dozen dude ranches.

**Van Horn (Pop. 1,893)**

If you're not planning on pitching a tent at Guadalupe Mountains National Park, Van Horn is a perfect base camp. Some decent hotels are available, and the El Capitan Hotel restaurant cooks up one of the best steaks in Texas.

**Brackettville (Pop. 1,642)**

Home of Fort Clark Springs and the Seminole Indian Scout Cemetery, this town offers excellent access to the Kickapoo Caverns.

**Marathon (Pop. 365)**

Home of the well-known, singularly located Gage Hotel and a great stop on the way to Big Bend National Park, the town has a good coffee shop and a few nice galleries and boutiques.

**Atlanta (Pop: 5,433)**

This small town is the birthplace of UFC kickboxer Andrea "KGB" Lee, pioneering Black aviator Bessie Coleman, and country music legend Tracy Lawrence. Ellen DeGeneres graduated high school there in 1976.

# RIVER ROAD
## FROM LAJITAS TO PRESIDIO

This is the premier road trip in Texas, and it packs a wallop. Except for El Paso, folks who dwell in every other big city in Texas are somewhat insulated from the practical reality of living in a border state. A large percentage of these people avoid spending time on the border, which is really a shame. It might disavow them of some of their misconceptions.

The "River Road," also known as El Camino del Rio, runs right through the southern reaches of the relatively new 311,000-acre Big Bend Ranch State Park. This spectacular route is stark, dramatic, and picturesque. There's never a dull moment as the road climbs, twists, dips, and drops though the landscape, revealing startling vistas, tepee-shelter rest stops, hoodoo hikes, abandoned structures, a movie set, and sneak peeks of the elusive Rio Grande. Warnings not to cross the river demarcation abound, but gringos do it on tourist larks every day. The restored Fort Leaton is worth a stop, and the short but sensational Closed Canyon is a must-see, even when the temperatures are pushing 107 degrees.

tpwd.texas.gov/state-parks/big-bend-ranch

tpwd.texas.gov/state-parks/fort-leaton

# LOS EBANOS FERRY TERMINAL

There are few things Texans enjoy more than sticking their thumb in the eye of appointed or self-appointed arbiters of what's prim, proper, acceptable, or even advisable, and that's why crossing the Rio Grande at Los Ebanos is so awesome. Connecting Americans at the Rio Grande with Ciudad Diaz Ordaz in Mexico, the Los Ebanos Ferry is the only remaining hand-pulled ferry in the United States. Known as El Chalan, the three-vehicle barge links the state of Texas with the Mexican state of Tamaulipas. The ferry runs from 8:00 a.m. to 3:30 p.m., seven days a week. A US Border & Customs Service office operates on the American side of the ferry landing.

200 Flores St., Los Ebanos, TX 78565

US Border & Customs Service: (956) 485-1084

## INTREPID TEXAN

The National Butterfly Center (a private nature preserve operated by the North American Butterfly Association) is located 20 miles away (via US-83 W) adjacent to Bentsen-Rio Grande Valley State Park, near Mission, TX.

84

# NEW LONDON SCHOOL EXPLOSION

The state of Texas is no stranger to tragedies, mishaps, and catastrophic events, but the New London School Explosion on May 18, 1937, was particularly gut-wrenching and heartbreaking. At the time, the London School District was flush with oil and gas tax revenues, making it one of the wealthiest in the nation. In fact, at their home football games, the London Wildcats faced opponents on the first gridiron in Texas to have electric lights. For some reason, however, school officials had foregone a traditional boiler heating system for six dozen gas heaters, and the gas pipes were leaking. When a shop instructor switched on an electric sander at 3:17 p.m., the resultant spark ignited the gas-air mixture. The massive explosion that followed killed more than 300 students and teachers and injured another 300 people. Legendary Texas journalist Walter Cronkite's coverage of the explosion was his first national story.

London Museum & Cafe
10690 Main St., Overton, TX 75684
(903) 895-4602, nlsd.net/Museum.htm

### INTREPID TEXAN

One wall of the London Museum features a telegram expressing condolences from Adolf Hitler.

# BIG THICKET NATIONAL PRESERVE

One of the most biodiverse areas in the world outside the tropics, the 105,000-acre Big Thicket National Preserve is best explored on foot and offers 40 miles of trails to pursue that end. Home to 85 species of trees (including oak, sweet gum, beech, magnolia, pine, tupelo, and holly), the patchwork park protects 26 species of fern, 20 species of orchid, 185 species of birds, more than 50 species of reptiles, and at least four carnivorous plants.

During the Civil War, a considerable number of East Texas dissidents hid out in the Big Thicket to avoid being drafted by the Confederacy into what they considered "a rich man's war and a poor man's fight." In the spring of 1865, a Confederate captain burned down more than 3,000 acres of the Thicket in an unsuccessful attempt to flush out the real rebels.

Over the years, parts of the Thicket have sheltered destitute families and purported "wild men," and some suggest it even provides a safe haven for Bigfoot. Bring beef jerky just in case.

Big Thicket National Preserve Visitors Center
6102 FM 420, Kountze, TX 77625
(409) 951-6700, nps.gov/bith/index.htm

# INDIANOLA

Located on Matagorda Bay in Calhoun County, the ghost town of Indianola lies near where French Explorer Robert Cavelier, Sieur de LaSalle, landed in 1685, mistaking the bay there for the mouth of the Mississippi River. Indianola was founded in 1846 but demolished by a hurricane in 1875. The local citizenry rebuilt the town and the courthouse, but it was destroyed again by another hurricane in 1886 and subsequently abandoned.

Not much of the Indianola community remains today, but a historical marker is near the original town site as well as a 40-foot-tall granite statue of LaSalle overlooking the bay. The foundation of the second Calhoun County courthouse of Indianola can still be seen out in the water at low tide.

## INTREPID TEXAN

For an almost entirely primitive Gilligan-esque experience, the Matagorda Island Wildlife Management Area can be accessed by watercraft.

tpwd.texas.gov/huntwild/hunt/wma/find_a_wma/list/?id=48

# ROY ORBISON MUSEUM

In April 1963, Roy Orbison signed on to tour the UK with a new, young English band who called themselves the Beatles. Upon his arrival, he quickly realized that even though he was better known and had had more success than the young Liverpool quartet, they were being advertised as the main draw. On opening night in Glasgow, Orbison agreed to play first and, after a dazzling set, began playing encores. After the first several encores, the Beatles stood stupefied backstage. After listening to the raucous crowd chant "We Want Roy!" again, after Orbison's 14th encore, the Beatles practically dragged him off the stage. Orbison would go on to be a close friend of the Beatles and continue stealing the spotlight from other iconic bands he toured with, including the Rolling Stones and the Beach Boys. His genius is immortalized in various legendary rock-n-roll mainstays, including "Only the Lonely," "Running Scared," "Crying," "Pretty Woman," and "Blue Bayou."

Not too shabby for a quiet, unassuming young man born in the small town of Vernon and raised in the smaller West Texas town of Wink (which Orbison described as the "the middle of nowhere, 500 miles from everywhere"). Visitors come from all over the world to check out the little museum dedicated to him there, and so should we all. Call in advance to schedule a visit.

213 Hendricks Blvd., Wink, TX 79789
(432) 634-4873 or (432) 999-8838 (BY APPOINTMENT ONLY)

# ROBERT E. HOWARD MUSEUM

Author Robert E. Howard was born in Peaster, went to high school in Brownwood, attended Howard Payne College, and spent most of his adult life in the little town of Cross Plains. But from his small corner of West Texas, he conquered civilizations, particularly as his most famous character "Conan the Barbarian." In his short, prolific career, Howard wrote mostly for pulp magazines but basically pioneered the sword and sorcery genre and is rivaled only by J. R. R. Tolkien in terms of his influence in the field of fantasy fiction. He was a friend and associate of horror writer H. P. Lovecraft and influenced legendary East Texas writer Joe R. Lansdale.

Today, Howard's Conan enjoys a pop-culture iconography not unlike that of Tarzan, Dracula, or Sherlock Holmes, and every summer, Cross Plains hosts a Robert E. Howard Days gathering.

625 SW Fifth St., Cross Plains, TX 76443
(254) 725-4993 or (254) 725-7377 (BY APPOINTMENT ONLY)

# LEMON JEFFERSON MEMORIAL CEMETERY

The grave in this cemetery (formerly known as the Wortham Negro Cemetery) that folks usually come to visit is the final resting place of blues legend and facility namesake, Blind Lemon Jefferson. Though he typically gets less attention than his disciples, Huddie "Leadbelly" Ledbetter and Aaron Thibeaux "T-Bone" Walker, Jefferson was the first successful blues artist in America and is recognized as the Father of Texas blues. Jefferson's influence on popular music is probably impossible to quantify, especially in terms of later blues and rock artists, such as Sam "Lightnin'" Hopkins, Louis Armstrong, B. B. King, Carl Perkins, Bob Dylan, Jefferson Airplane, and the Beatles.

Jefferson died on December 19, 1929, but his exact cause of death is unknown. When his body was returned to Texas, it was interred in an unmarked grave in Wortham. In 1967, Jefferson finally received a memorial.

When fans of Texas rock legend Buddy Holly visit his final resting place in Lubbock, they're encouraged to place guitar picks on his grave, but on Jefferson's gravestone and echoed in his haunting, classic 1927 song "See That My Grave Is Kept Clean," he makes his wishes abundantly clear:

Located on the west side of State Hwy. 14 just north of
Freestone County Rd. 1010

Balanced Rock on Grapevine Trail
Photo courtesy of E. R. Bills

# PHOTO OPS

# COWBOY CHRIST

A gravesite in the Evergreen Cemetery near Paris, Texas, features a statue of Jesus (or an angel) that is wearing cowboy boots under his mantel. Whether you're a born-again Christian or borne away by alternate metaphysical interpretations, the booted deity (or disciple) is a nice touch, which will either make you smile and nod or smile and shake your head. It's a Texas thing, regardless.

560 Evergreen St., Paris, TX 75460
(903) 784-6750

### INTREPID TEXAN

Not far away is the Paris, Texas, Eiffel Tower. Constructed in 1993, this 65-foot-tall replica is topped with a red cowboy hat.

91

# BALANCED ROCK
## (BIG BEND)

The 2.2-mile round-trip Grapevine Hills Trail at the Big Bend National Park doesn't have the star quality of the South Rim hike, the sex appeal of the Lost Mine Trail climb, or the stark beauty of the Santa Elena Canyon Trail, but what it lacks in drama, it makes up for in pleasing serendipity. The moderate hike ends with three boulders perfectly placed to create a triangular window. The formation makes for decent shade and an almost comic interjection into an otherwise forbidding landscape.

92

# STEVIE RAY VAUGHAN STATUE

Stevie Ray Vaughan's first album, *Texas Flood* (1983), couldn't have been more appropriately titled. With his band, Double Trouble, Vaughan stormed the American music scene with a deluge of six-string virtuosity, practically single-handedly restoring the blues to the fore of the rock and roll music conversation and boosting the careers of neglected legends, such as B. B. King, Etta James, and Buddy Guy. Vaughan's bold, unshakable riffs fueled such signature hits as "Cold Shot," "Lovestruck Baby," "The Sky is Crying," "Pride and Joy," "Life by the Drop," "Little Wing," "The House is Rockin,'" "Look at Little Sister," "Tightrope," (too many to name), and also lent considerable weight to David Bowie's best-selling album *Let's Dance* (1983). Then, of course, there's SRV's rendition of Hendrix's "Voodoo Child," where he arguably out-Jimi-ed Jimi himself.

At the time of his untimely demise in a helicopter crash in Wisconsin on August 27, 1990, Vaughan had inspired millions of fans and won the admiration of a number of his fellow guitar greats, including Keith Richards, Eric Clapton, and Jeff Beck. His influence is still expanding, but the sky isn't crying as much as it should.

Auditorium Shores
Ann and Roy Butler Hike and Bike Trail, Austin, TX 78704

93

# EARL CAMPBELL STATUE

Three years after winning the Heisman Trophy and becoming the first pick in the 1978 NFL draft by the Houston Oilers, running back Earl Campbell was enshrined as an Official State Hero of Texas. His only three predecessors, Sam Houston, Davy Crockett, and Stephen F. Austin, had all been dead for more than a hundred years.

In a football state, Campbell was a man among boys at every level, leading John Tyler High School to a state championship and the Texas Longhorns to a national title game. At the pro level, Campbell's combination of breakaway speed, agility, and power earned him NFL Offensive Rookie of the Year honors in 1978 and the Offensive Player of the Year award in each of his first three seasons. He also won the Associated Press MVP Award in 1979, was a five-time Pro Bowler, a three-time 1st Team All-Pro, led the NFL in rushing from 1978 to 1980, and rushing touchdowns from 1979 to 1980.

Campbell was named to the NFL Hall of Fame in 1991, and the 9-foot-tall likeness of him sits in the southwest corner of Darrell K Royal-Texas Memorial Stadium.

405 E. 23rd St., Austin, TX 78712

# AURORA CEMETERY HISTORICAL MARKER

Who doesn't want a picture of themselves standing at the site of the first documented UFO crash site in the United States?

The first official sighting of a "flying" saucer didn't occur in Roswell, New Mexico, in early July 1947, and it wasn't conjured up on *The Day the Earth Stood Still* movie set in Century City, California, a few years later. New Mexico and Hollywood were late to the party. The first flying saucer was spotted by a farmer named John Martin in North Texas on Tuesday, January 22, 1878, and 19 years later, the first alien aircraft reportedly made unscheduled contact with Earth in the form of a spectacular crash on April 17, 1897. The pilot, who was assumed to be Martian, did not survive, and the citizens of Aurora respectfully interred him the next day, Easter morning, at their local cemetery.

507 Cemetery Rd., Aurora, TX 76078

## INTREPID TEXAN

The grave of the legendary songwriter behind Willie Nelson's country western ballad "Pancho and Lefty" is just 10 miles south at the Dido Cemetery in Pecan Acres. The Fort Worth native's name was Townes Van Zandt, and his inscription reads "To Live's to Fly."

95

# LIGHTNIN' HOPKINS STATUE

The state of Texas's impact in the realm of blues music is no less seminal than its role in rock. The first major American blues artist was Coutchman native Blind Lemon Jefferson, and he mentored Louisiana legend Huddie "Leadbelly" Ledbetter in Dallas's Deep Ellum. Texas also produced Blind Willie Johnson, Aaron "T-Bone" Walker, Sippie Wallace, Clarence "Gatemouth" Brown, Albert Collins, Johnny "Guitar" Watson, Delbert McClinton, and Stevie Ray Vaughan. Besides Vaughan, the only Lone Star blues master who has a statue is Centerville native Sam "Lightnin'" Hopkins, who was a major influence on Jimi Hendrix, Billy Gibbons (of ZZ Top), and Creedence Clearwater Revival. At least a half-dozen other blues pioneers ought to have their own statues here in Texas, but we certainly won't turn our nose up at the one we have of Hopkins in Crockett.

200th block of S. 3rd St. in Crockett, in a small park
between Fannin and Goliad Avenues

# GUADALUPE PEAK

Guadalupe Peak is the highest point in Texas, and getting there is no easy task. From the Pine Springs Visitor Center in the Guadalupe Mountains National Park, the 8.8-mile round-trip hike to the 8,749-peak involves a strenuous 2,927-foot gain in elevation, but once you arrive you're greeted by a steel pyramid at the summit and fantastic views all around, especially on a clear day. A photo or selfie with the commemorative spire in the background at this rarefied perch is quite something and an accomplishment you'll be glad you captured. And don't forget to retrieve the notebook from the small ammo box at the base of the steel spire and record your thoughts for future fellow climbers.

400 Pine Canyon Dr., Salt Flat, TX 79847
(915) 828-3251, nps.gov/gumo/index.htm

## INTREPID TEXAN

In 1982, three paraplegic climbers in wheelchairs reached the summit of Guadalupe Peak after five days. Where there's a will, there's a way.

# SAM HOUSTON STATUE

The 67-foot statue of Sam Houston standing on the east side of I-45 in Huntsville is the Lone Star state's Mount Rushmore. For Texas, Houston was George Washington, Thomas Jefferson (Houston was our first and third president), and Abraham Lincoln. Three out of four ain't bad.

Before Houston was a general, president, senator, or governor for the Republic or State of Texas, he was a Cherokee Nation citizen known as Colonneh, meaning "the Raven." He was also a keen contrarian. Though a Southern slave owner, he opposed Texas secession from the Union, warning that "the soil of our beloved South will drink deep the previous blood of our sons and brethren." And although he couldn't convince his fellow political representatives and citizens that they were committing a grave mistake in joining the Confederacy, he refused an offer from Lincoln to command a Union army to put down the Confederate forces in Texas. He couldn't stomach bearing arms against his fellow Texans.

## INTREPID TEXAN

Howard Hughes, another Texas giant, is buried at Glenwood Cemetery in downtown Houston an hour south on Interstate 45 (depending on the traffic).

Lighthouse Peak
Photo courtesy of Thomas Shahan

# LIGHTHOUSE PEAK

A distinctive "hoodoo" formation near Capitol Peak in Palo Duro Canyon State Park, the Lighthouse stands three miles off the main park road. The Lighthouse Trail climbs 900 feet and offers little shade but is relatively moderate. The best place to get a picture is where the trail flattens out at the end of the first rise of the two-level ascent at the end of the hike.

Palo Duro Canyon State Park
11450 State Hwy. Park Rd. 5, Canyon, TX 79015
(806) 488-2227, tpwd.texas.gov/state-parks/palo-duro-canyon

## INTREPID TEXAN

The hike is moderate, but there are also two or three horseback riding outfits that offer transport to the Lighthouse Peak.

# BUDDY HOLLY STATUE

In the same way that American blues spread from the mastery of such artists as Blind Lemon Jefferson, rock and roll branched out from the artistry of Buddy Holly. John Lennon and Paul McCartney saw Holly when they were teenagers and based their music on his, later offering tribute to Holly's band the Crickets by naming their band the Beatles. Holly's *The Chirping Crickets* was the first album Eric Clapton ever purchased. At the age of 13, Elton John wore horn-rimmed glasses to imitate Holly, even though he didn't need them. Bruce Springsteen claimed that in the early days, he always played Buddy Holly before he went on because it kept him honest. Keith Richards put Holly's impact best when he said, "He's in everybody."

Holly's songlist, which includes "That'll Be the Day," "Oh Boy," and "True Love Ways," is timeless, and the raw footage of Holly and the Crickets performing "Peggy Sue" on the Ed Sullivan Show on December 1, 1957, still gives folks chills. Holly's career came to an abrupt end on February 3, 1959, when he, J. P. "Big Bopper" Richardson, and Ritchie Valens were killed in a plane crash northwest of Mason City, Iowa.

1824 Crickets Ave., Lubbock, TX 79401

## INTREPID TEXAN

The phrase "the day the music died" in Don McLean's "American Pie" refers to the aforementioned 1959 plane crash. A losing coin toss over who got to fly in the plane or ride on the bus saved Waylon Jennings's life.

100

# INVASION OF THE PICTURE SNAPPERS

Five species of blue legume grow in Texas: *Lupinus subcarnosus, Lupinus havardii*, *Lupinus concinnus*, *Lupinus perennis*, and *Lupinus plattensis*. Alternatively called a wolf flower, buffalo clover, and el conejo, Texans obsess over them every April. Otherwise normal folks begin pulling off on the sides of state highways or just plowing into the roadside gravel of farm roads. They jump out with cameras or phones with cameras and begin supervising poses and instructing their models, who vary in age from toddler to preteen and stand on two legs or four. The models sit, lie, smile, hug, and sometimes bark among the bluebonnets—the state flower.

And the cameras keep rolling.

The Devil's Watering Hole at Inks Lake State Park
Photo courtesy of E. R. Bills

# SUGGESTED ITINERARIES

## WEEKEND GETAWAY

**Jefferson:** This Marion County treasure (#59) near the eastern edge of Texas is tough to beat. The weekly Ghost Walk conducted in the well-preserved downtown is wildly entertaining (even for skeptics). Then, there's the haunted Excelsior House hotel, which you can test your mettle by staying in, and the Grove, which is the most haunted place in Texas. The town is also home to the nostalgic Jefferson General Store, the fascinating Jefferson Historic Museum, and one of the last remaining Carnegie Libraries (that's still in operation) in Texas. And it's easy access to Caddo Lake (#28), Lake O' the Pines (#39), Bigfoot (#18), and the fickle little town of Uncertain.

**Galveston:** A Texas quasi-Mardi Gras without the gratuitous nudity or regurgitation 365 days a year that features the sea, the seawall (#6), the Pleasure Pier (with games and rides), the beach, the Strand, eclectic shops, the wondrous Bishop's Palace, the Moody Gardens and awesome Aquarium Pyramid, the Galveston Bookstore (#24), the Galveston Island State Park, the Mosquito Café, and convenient ferry access to the Bolivar Peninsula and Bolivar Lighthouse.

**Inks Lake State Park:** A hill country gem that features camping, biking, hiking, swimming (#31), cliff diving, great fishing, and places like the Blanco River (#31), Longhorn Caverns (#34), Pedernales Falls State Park, Cooper's Barbecue (#70), and the grim Dead Man's Hole in striking distance.

**San Antonio:** The host with the most traditional history, Tex-Mex eats, and ancillary must-dos. The River Walk (#3), the Alamo (#47), the historic Menger Hotel Bar (#23), the Natural Bridge Caverns (#34), The Twig (#24) in the Pearl District, El Milagrito Café (#69), La Musica de San Anto Mural (featuring native legend Doug Sahm and others), the San Antonio Stock Show & Rodeo (#5) in February, and the 10-day Fiesta San Antonio in late April. Victory or Death!

## THREE-DAY WEEKEND GETAWAY

**Fort Davis:** Great West Texas town that makes a perfect base camp for the McDonald Observatory (#11), the namesake fort historic site (#55), the Davis Mountains State Park, Kit Carson Rock and the incredible Scenic Loop Drive, and situates you within striking distance of the San Solomon Springs (#31), Alpine (which features Front Street Books [#24]), and Marfa (#1). Plus, if you're traveling from DFW, you can make short stops at the Odessa Meteor Crater (#45), Monahans Sandhills (#33), and the ghost town of Kent (#10).

**Palo Duro Canyon State Park:** Second only to the Grand Canyon in the US, Palo Duro features 30 miles of hiking trails, horseback riding opportunities, the Lighthouse Peak rock formation (#98), and proximity to Canyon, Texas, home to the Panhandle-Plains Historical Museum and the Pioneer Amphitheatre. The park is also a half hour or less from Cadillac Ranch (#14), top of Texas Pro Wrestling (#25), the 72-ounce Big Texan Challenge (#21), Ozymandias on the Plains, and "The Town without a Frown," Happy, Texas.

**Corpus Christi:** Like San Antonio, Corpus Christi packs a punch. Namely, the Texas State Aquarium (#4), the 60-mile Padre Island National Seashore (#30), Laguna Adventures Floating Cabin Rentals (#39), the Mirador de la Flor monument to Tejano music superstar Selena Quintanilla Perez, the USS Lexington Museum on the Bay, Mustang Island State Park, and neat options such as Glow Rows and the Texas Surf Museum.

**Austin:** It's expensive, crowded, overly trendy, and over traffic-jammed, but unrivaled in many ways. With SXSW and the Texas Book Festival (#8), the Broken Spoke (#9), Book People (#24), Barton Springs (#31), the state capitol (#53), Angie's (#69), Franklin Barbecue (#70), Texas Chili Parlor (#77), SRV (#92), the Tyler Rose (#93), Lake Travis, Congress Avenue Bridge bat viewing, the Driskill, the *Austin Chronicle*, *Slacker* bohemia, and on and on, the Capitol City is "Alright, alright, alright."

# ONE-WEEK VACATION GETAWAY

**Big Bend National Park:** A whole week is a good primer (#26) and affords you a signature opportunity for an Textreme feat (#43); a Buster Keaton-esque photo op (#91); hikes on the Lost Mine Trail or to Ernst Tinaja, Santa Elena Canyon, and so on; jaunts to Marfa (#1) or Marathon (#81); a drive down the River Road from Lajitas to Presidio (#82); the Big Bend Ranch State Park; Fort Leaton; Presidio (#82); and the ghost town of Shafter (#10). Stay in the Chisos Basin Lodge or camp close to the river. Visit Terlingua for the namesake Trading Post and the Starlight Theatre Restaurant. Get away from the glare of civilization and gaze at our peace of the Milky Way at night. Plan ahead.

**Go Indigenous:** Watch out for Chupacabras, of course (#18), but base camp out of Del Rio ( #81) or Seminole Canyon, and visit the Fate Bell Shelter (#49), the White Shaman (#50), Kickapoo Caverns (#34), the remarkable Devil's River (#35), Brackettville and the Seminole Scout Cemetery (#81), and the Devil's Sinkhole (#36). Nothing is close to anything, and expanses separate everything. Take plenty of water and food. Watch your fuel tank, and research before you take your Tesla. This is not for most "tourists" in a conventional sense. This is for the explorers.

**Dallas-Fort Worth Metroplex:** Once you crack it open, it's an egg with two yolks. With Arlington connecting them, Dallas is Rome to Fort Worth's Florence, and both abound with staggering must-sees. In Big D, visit Big Tex (#12), the Sixth Floor Museum (#54) and Dealey Plaza, see the Dallas Mavericks or Stars (#13), catch a movie in the Texas Theater (#19), stay classy at the Midnight Rambler (#23), get your drink or eat on at lower Greenville Avenue, check out Deep Ellum, and more. On the Cowtown side (Tarrant County), see the Dallas Cowboys and Texas Rangers play (#13 in Arlington), take in a weekly championship rodeo (#5), wet your whistle at the White Elephant Saloon (#23), some wrasslin' (#25) or something else at Dickies Arena, track the Lake Worth Monster (#18), experience the Stockyards (#52), visit the incredible art collections (#17), eat at Goldee's Barbecue (#70) or Drew's (#73), or sneak off and look for the spaceman's grave in Aurora (#94). The 9th and 13th highest populated cities in the US are 30 minutes apart and provide access to all the above and so much more.

**Padre Island National Seashore:** Consider that the longest stretch of undeveloped beach in America and the longest undeveloped barrier island on the planet is at your flip-flopped toe tips for a low weekly cost per vehicle. Plan for seven days of salt life with a mile or five to yourself. If you bring a four-wheel-drive vehicle, explore the entire length of this unspoiled paradise. See the Port Mansfield Channel that separates North Padre from South Padre Island. See the SS *Nicaragua* out in the water at low-tide (but don't swim out to it—the rusty metal is sharp). Bring your own food and water (and plenty of ice), camp under the stars, take solar showers, surf fish, body surf, collect shells at Big or Little Seashell Beach, or just survey the strange detritus that sometimes washes up on the shoreline. There are very few people 25 to 30 miles down, so live in a bathing suit and hoard seaside solitude. There is no power, so bring a portable generator if you like. There is no private or public privy past the Malaquite Visitor Center, so bring a small shovel (and maybe even an outdoor privacy/bath tent). This is the real deal. If you go very far, you'll have no cell service. This is as close to a *Survivor* episode as most people ever want to get. Plan ahead. Bring plenty of sunblock, a first aid kit, and watch out for endangered sea turtles.

Janis Joplin
Photo courtesy of Wikimedia Commons

L & J Cafe in El Paso
Photo courtesy of E. R. Bills

# INDEX

Art outside the South Austin Museum of Popular Culture
Carol M. Highsmith America/Library of Congress

Katherine Stinson with her biplane
Photo courtesy of Library of Congress